Russia – the State of Reforms

Study report of the Institute of Europe
coordinated by Sergei A. Karaganov

Strategies
and Options
for Europe

Bertelsmann Foundation Publishers
Gütersloh 1993

Die Deutsche Bibliothek – Cataloguing-in-Publication Data

Karaganov, Sergej A.:
Russia – the state of reforms ; study report of the Institute of Europe /
Sergei A. Karaganov. – Gütersloh : Bertelsmann Foundation Publ., 1993
  (Strategies and options for Europe)
  ISBN 3-89204-083-4

© 1993 Bertelsmann Foundation Publishers, Gütersloh
Project director: Dirk Rumberg
Editor: Brigitte Neuparth
Production editor: Sabine Klemm
Cover design: HTG Werbeagentur, Bielefeld
Cover photo: © GLOBUS-Kartendienst, Hamburg u. dpa, Frankfurt/Agence France
Layout and typesetting: Mohndruck Graphische Betriebe GmbH, Gütersloh
Print: Gütersloher Druckservice
ISBN: 3-89204-083-4

Table of Contents

Preface 5

Introduction 7

1. Disintegration of a Single Political Space and
   the Emergence of the New Balance of Forces 12

2. Ethno-Political Conflicts on the Territory
   of the Former USSR 20

3. Economic Space of the Former USSR and
   the Prospects for Market Reforms 27

4. The Military and Political Aspects 35

5. The Political Situation in Russia 49

6. The Political Situation in the CIS Countries 59

7. Interstate Relations in Post-Soviet Politics 67

8. The CIS: a Year After 73

9. The Alternative Scenarios 78

Tables and Charts 88
The Author 92
The Project Partners 93
The Publications 94

Preface

For years to come, Russia and her neighbors in the Commonwealth of Independent States will lag in the process of transformation towards democracy and market economy. Uncertainties prevail about the ability of policy makers to maintain a reform momentum and to secure political and social peace at the same time.

Neither Russia, which is confronted with problems of its own, and at the same time is seen to be the prime mover with regard to the political and economic development of the CIS as a whole, nor the West possess readymade solutions and strategies designed to contribute to a stabilization of the Russian Federation. In the long run short-term assistance will not be enough. On the other hand, the Russian government has not as yet managed to present the West with a comprehensive plan that would be worth supporting in financial terms.

The study by Professor Sergei A. Karaganov, Deputy Director at the Institute of Europe of the Russian Academy of Sciences in Moscow, present a sober analysis of the numerous Russian problems and, over and above this, provides us with a number of carefully refined concepts with which he runs through the various developmental alternatives open to Russia and the CIS in the future. The book examines the political, regional and economic factors that may contribute to instability in Russia and to a further decline of the Commonwealth of Independent States to the level of political insignificance. As a result of the uncertainties, the West is also faced with a number of unpredictable imponderables in the military field. Whether the former Soviet republics will act in a predictable manner remains to be seen. The study enumerates possible constellations in the division of power, considers trends in the future development, and describes possible solutions that have not as yet become part of the academic debate.

The study was carried out under the auspices of "Strategies and Options for the Future of Europe", the joint research project of the

Bertelsmann Foundation and the Research Group on European Affairs at the Johannes Gutenberg-University, Mainz. Its approach to the subject is based on the project's systematic goal, which is to appraise and analyze the problems of European politics, to evolve the aims and criteria for a solution from a political science viewpoint, and to extrapolate suggestions for the political decision-making process.

My thanks are due to Cornelius Ochmann and Markus Klaes, at the Research Group on European Affairs who have prepared the text for publication and to Antje Göttges who served as language editor.

Professor Dr. Werner Weidenfeld
Member of the Board of the
Bertelsmann Foundation
Head of the Research Group on
European Affairs at the
University of Mainz

Introduction
Werner Weidenfeld

The total collapse of the power structures in Eastern Europe has led many people, and not only in the Western community of nations, to ask how one can best avoid the emergence of a political power vacuum in the states of the former Soviet Union. The future economic and regional development of Russia and the Commonwealth of Independent States is also of considerable importance to the West. The study concentrates on the problems that have arisen as a result of the break-up of the Soviet Union. In contrast to previous Western assessments of the situation, the regionalization of Russia and the alienation between the states of the CIS are given top priority. For this reason the analysis of the effects of a further decentralization in Russia and the increasing autonomy of the member states of the CIS is of importance for an understanding of future political developments. Sergei Karaganov gives a graphic description of the tensions that have arisen, particularly in the Russian political arena, after the upheavals in Eastern Europe.

In this context the study depicts the situation with which the new states were confronted after the demise of the Soviet Union. Secondly, it analyzes the internal political situation in Russia and the relationship between Russia and the CIS. There follows a brief description of the relations between its various member states. The present study ends with a number of scenarios of the possible future development of the Commonwealth of Independent States and of the Russian Federation.

Sergei Karaganov identifies many of the problems and the central issues that are uppermost in the minds of the world community with regard to Russia and the CIS. By way of an introduction to the problems of post-Soviet politics, he examines the origins and reasons for the present conflicts and suggests certain alternative developments.

Points of Departure

The break-up of the Soviet Union and the creation of a commonwealth of states went hand in hand with the emergence of problems that had been suppressed by the central power for many decades. The problems currently to be encountered in the Commonwealth of Independent States have come to the surface in an unusually violent manner. The attentive observer cannot overlook the fact that day-to-day political reports in the Western media often deal with crises in Russia. These crises are not only of an economic and political nature, but are sometimes also due to ethnic and cultural conflicts. People who for decades were neighbours, colleagues at work and friends have suddenly started to shoot at each other. The reasons for this are almost impossible to understand for Western Europeans, mainly because we have not had problems of this kind for over forty years. Today no one can predict for how long the current Russian government under President Boris Yeltsin is likely to remain in power. No one is willing to predict the future of the Commonwealth of Independent States. Everything is in a state of flux, and the situation is complicated by the fact that the interests of the protagonists are so closely interlinked.

Thus the West regards the future development of Russia and the CIS with a great deal of interest, and differing assessments of the future of the Russian polity are currently the subject of debate. The West's greatest worry is that the internal and external stability of the Russian Federation will deteriorate even further, thus casting doubt on whether Russia can retain the leadership of the CIS. In this connection there is the question of the extent to which Russia will be in a position to exercise an influence on the bitter conflicts raging within the boundaries of the former Soviet Union, and the effect that this will have on the ongoing security situation. The West in general and the Europeans in particular do not possess a plan of action in the event of a further destabilization of the internal political situation in the Russian Federation. Closely linked with the development of internal politics in Russia is the future of the CIS. Here again, if Russia is no longer in a position to assume a leading role and the danger of a political vacuum becomes acute, the West possesses no variable alternatives.

These are only some of the scenarios that present themselves to the student of international politics. Whilst it is not feasible to give a comprehensive answer to all possible developments, the present study suggests a number of interesting approaches that will not doubt become part of the international debate.

The Problem Areas

In order to be able to provide answers to these numerous and highly sensitive problem areas, Karaganov focusses on the following four areas:
a) politics
b) economic policy
c) military and security policies and
d) the ethnic and cultural conflicts.

Karaganov examines these areas with regard to Russia, the Commonwealth of Independent States and the surviving structures of the former Soviet Union, so that a pattern emerges on the basis of which the reader can understand the developmental phases and the resultant problems.

a) The political scenario. This defines and describes the correlations between the three remaining political power bases – the surviving political apparatus of the Soviet Union, the new political institutions of Russia, and the political structures of the CIS – and the resultant political constraints. The break-up of the Soviet Union created a new set of political parameters. At the same time, however, the old political power structures were not completely abolished. The three groups, which sometimes intersect and which are sometimes quite distinct, all pursue different interests. This leads to unpredictable conflicts on the political decision-making level.

b) Economic policy was dealt an unexpected blow by the downfall of the USSR's socialist system. The old economic order collapsed all at once, and the new states were forced to embark on a complete restructuring of their mutual economic relations. This restructuring is currently taking place on a multilateral and on a bilateral basis. Goods and merchandise that in the past were able to cross the borders of the republics without let or hindrance suddenly required export and import licences. The different economic power of the various former Soviet republics and the differing natural resources at their disposal constitute another potentially explosive source of conflict.

c) For the West, security and military policies are certainly of significance and should not be neglected. In order to integrate the CIS and Russia into the international peace and security framework, the West needs to know who is actually in control of weapons and armaments in the various states and regions of the former Soviet Union. Furthermore, it would be useful to know whether there is a tendency in certain regions to attract the attention of the international community by threatening to use violence. The military pot-

ential of the various regions and the CIS states may well come to be seen as a means of settling border disputes.
d) Ethnic and cultural conflicts are closely connected with certain aspects of security and military policy, especially when they reach a certain intensity. The origins of and reasons for the increasing number of ethnic and cultural conflicts deserve to be examined in detail, and their progress and possible growth need to be kept under constant review.

Developments in Russia: Some Scenarios

The reader will no doubt benefit from the analysis of the present state of affairs in Russia and the CIS states. However, the question remains of what is likely to happen in the immediate future, and of how the situation will develop in the coming months and years in Russia and the CIS states. In fact, are there any alternatives to the present political situations? Sergei Karaganov addresses himself to these problems in his last chapter, "The Alternative Scenarios".

A total of eleven different models attempt to predict the future of the Commonwealth of Independent States and the Russian Federation. Some of course are more likely to materialize than others. The models which seem to me to be most disturbing in the present political situation – because the may very well come true – are, briefly, as follows:

The first scenario envisages the so-called "Citizens Union" around Volsky and Rutzkoy taking over the leadership in Russia. This group derives much of its support from the upper decision-making echelons of politics, trade and commerce, and the academic world. It remains to be seen whether the incumbent government and President Yeltsin can reach some kind of modus vivendi with this group and thus remain in power. Karaganov believes the first scenario to be the most plausible alternative to the present political situation,

The second scenario envisages the "red-brown alternative" seizing power. Its supporters are apparatchiks and diehard communists who are strictly against further economic reform and the democratization of Russia. If this alliance under the leadership of Parliamentary President Chasbulatov came to power, the consequences might include the isolation of Russia in foreign policy terms, and a renewed strengthening of the military establishment. It might also lead to a kind of civil war in certain parts of Russia.

The third alternative is another military coup, this time in support of the President. Even if it is impossible to determine on which side the military stands, it may be assumed that it would come down on the side of Yeltsin. Naturally this would change the internal balance of power. If a coup were to take place in support of the President, it would be unrealistic to imagine that the process of democratization would in future continue to proceed at the same pace. Similarly, economic progress would grind to a halt. There would be a renewed emphasis on the military-industrial complex. The foreign policy implications of this situation are unpredictable. Support for Yeltsin might materialize, though international isolation would also be a possibility in view of the fact that the proponents of strictly authoritarian policies would gain the upper hand.

The wide range of hypotheses on the future of Russia and the Commonwealth of Independent States presented here demonstrates that the former Soviet Union is currently on the threshold of a new stage in the process of transformation development. Sergei Karaganov's book is designed to help us to become acquainted with and understand both the problems of transformation and the possibilities or opportunities open to the West. In the final analyses, it will help the West to formulate a coherent strategy.

1. Disintegration of a Single Political Space and the Emergence of the New Balance of Forces

Reasons of Disintegration

Disintegration has been the prevailing and most steady trend in the politics on the territory of the former USSR in recent years. It surfaced in various processes: the breakup of the Soviet Union, the "regionalization" of Russia and some other republics of the former USSR (Ukraine, Georgia, Moldova, etc.), the escalation of ethnic conflicts. All these developments may be summed up in the following formula: due to the breakup of the centralized power system, the entire political setup of the former USSR is being restructured.

As far as the Soviet Union was essentially a single giant corporation, the crush of its controlling unit left its key elements autonomous. These key elements were not the former quasi-state entities (Union and Autonomous Republics), but those who had real local power: the regional political elites.

The local centers of power began to form long before the Gorbachevian perestroika. The origins go back to the 1960s, when the Soviet political system started to evolve from Iosif Stalin's unitarianism to a more flexible model of the Nikita Khruschev and Leonid Brezhnev years. This model, underpinned by the cadres infrastructure of the Communist Party, put forward the key participants of the Soviet internal politics: the ministries for economic branches and the local power structures, notably the Oblast Committees of the CPSU. "You are masters of the country!", Constantin Chernenko claimed wholeheartedly addressing the First Secretaries of the Oblast Party Committees at the first conference he held after being elected General Secretary.

In Gorbachev's days this process of forging local political elites was dramatically accelerated. By fall 1991 it had resulted in an almost complete degeneration of the traditional Soviet unitary power structure so that the elimination of the "branch ministries" and Yeltsin's ban on the Communist Party did not lead to a complete power vacuum in the localities, as one could have expected. Starting from this point, the authority has been increasingly taken over by local elites who exert the strongest influence (though not always openly) on the post-Soviet political life.

Local elites have emerged (and continue to develop) in various regions and usually from the same social elements:
1. **The traditional clan and tribal system** that is most representative of the regions' history and culture. Despite the "internationalist" indoctrination, the clan relations were well preserved over the Soviet period (especially in the Caucasus and the Asian part of the former USSR) by finding a place in the communist power structures.
2. **The former party functionaries** who have retained extensive connections on the entire territory of the former USSR and still make up a sort of common cadres network. The authorities in certain regions (including those that are deemed "democratic") are almost completely staffed by the former nomenclatura. For example, the composition of the Nizhny Novgorod Oblast Administration under Yeltsin's protégé Boris Nemtsov has virtually not changed since the communist period.
3. **Heads of major industrial and agricultural enterprises of the regions.**
4. **Influential representatives of the private sector,** many of whom are connected with the old nomenclatura. This link goes back to the mid-1980s, when they covertly started investing state and party capital in joint ventures and private businesses. This social layer is sometimes merged with the local mafia.
5. **Local heads of law enforcement authorities, state security, and the army.**
6. **The representatives of a central republican authority** (in Russia – Representatives of the President, and Heads of Administration also appointed by him), a new element of local elites in the post-Soviet environment. As a rule, the majority of these representatives are incorporated into local elites and become a sort of captives. They play an important role in legitimatizing local elites and are sometimes used for applying pressure on the center.

Different Stages of Disintegration

Local elites emerge on certain territories, such as:
1. **Historically specific areas**, either in terms of their ethnic make-up (Chechnya, Daghestan, Turkic and Finno-Ugric lands of the Volga region, Yakut-Sakha, in the Russian Federation), or according to

local peculiarities in language, mentality, habits and ways (Galitia in Ukraine, Menghrelia in Georgia and the Ferghan Oblast in Uzbekistan).
2. **Wider traditional territories**: the Lvov area and adjacent lands that form the traditional community of West Ukraine, opposed to Central (Podolia), East and South Ukraine; Menghrelia, Guria and part of Abkhazia, that constitute West Georgia in contrast to East Georgia (Kartli); the Ferghan, Namanghan and Andizhan Oblasts, forming the wider Ferghan region as opposed to three other major areas of Uzbekistan: Tashkent, Samarkand-Bukhara, and Khiva.
3. The present deep economic crisis brings about the situation of economic austerity, barter trade and reliance on self-sufficiency. That is why local elites seeking autonomy emerge on **geographic and administrative territories** like Oblasts or economic regions. This is especially true for Russia and Ukraine. The main formative feature of the local elites is the control over natural resources (as seen in the regions producing raw materials like Komi and Yakut-Sakha Republics, Kuznetsk and Vorkuta coal fields, etc.) and over land the local authorities have hold over land that blocks the implementation of land reform).
4. A special kind of regional elites develop in **large cities, administrative and industrial centers** (Moscow, St. Peterbourg, Kiev, Sverdlovsk, Tomsk, Dnepropetrovsk, etc.). A stable local elite has emerged in Moscow under the previous (Gavriil Popov) and the present (Yuri Luzhkov) mayors.

Thus the territory of the former Soviet Union seen from the regional point of view is divided into a number of areas with steady, emerging, or latent centers of power. According to some calculations, there may be over 300 actual or potential local elites on the territory of the former USSR including the smallest on the district level. A substantial part of them is or may be seeking autonomy, and some may fuel instability and provoke regional conflicts.

The political situation in the post-Soviet world, strongly influenced by the local centers of power, is marked by the following key conflicts:
– conflicts between neighboring local political elites that can evolve into an open military conflict (regional ethnic conflicts are treated in Chapter 2).
– conflicts between local elites and the new republican centers that have assumed the functions of supreme authority. After the breakup of the Soviet Union the legitimacy, stability and efficiency of the republican centers are principally defined by their ability to maintain a balance of forces between the inner republican local el-

ites. However, it is much more difficult to maintain such a balance in the context of the paramount social and economic crisis and the lack of effective mechanisms of power. This brings about a situation in which the new republican centers (whose legitimacy is not yet secured because it has been traditionally coming from above, from Moscow, and not from the localities) are compelled to yield to the pressure of the local elites.

Russias Regionalization

After August 1991 the general trend of disintegration has been notably manifest **in Russia**. In federative relations it provoked the Autonomous Republics' and Autonomous Oblasts' struggle for full sovereignty and the regions' striving for autonomy. This process has been denoted "regionalization."

The new ambitions of local authorities and impulses towards regionalization of Russia appeared in the first weeks after the August coup. Ethnic divisions arose in multinational regions, and this resulted primarily in reshaping the state structure of Russia (the declarations of sovereignty in Tatarstan, Chechnya, Bashkortostan, etc.), and in sharpening ethnic territorial disputes (between Kabardins and Balkarians; Chechens, Ingushis, and Cossacks; Ingushis and Osetians; between ethnic groups in Daghestan, etc.). The tension increased between the native population of the national Autonomous Republics and the Russian-speaking population. New risks emerged, like the separation of the Russian-populated regions in Siberia and the Far East (the ideas of the Yenisei Republic and the Far Eastern Republic), or economic separatism that provoked political conflicts (the "blockade" of Moscow and St. Peterbourg).

Instead of attempting to maintain some kind of balance between local centers of power and offering a new conception of federative and regional politics, Moscow actually yielded to their demands and to the kind of politics they were imposing. Ceding wide economic and political powers to the local authorities, and hastily signing the Federative Treaty in April 1992, Moscow found itself in limbo.

Tatarstan and Chechnya refused to sign the treaty. The Tyumen Oblast was reluctant to the last minute, and signed the treaty with a number of substantial reservations. Thus the three strategically important regions with major reserves of oil and gas do not have any definite status within the Russian Federation. The Komi Republic (coal), Bashkortostan, and the Yakut-Sakha Republic (gold and diamonds) also joined the Federative Treaty on special terms. Exclusive economic rights and privileges were granted to Karelia, the Irkutsk Oblast and the Altai Republic. Next in line are the Buryat Republic, Kaliningrad, Chita, Amur, Arkhangelsk, Murmansk, Sverdlovsk and Chelyabinsk Oblasts, the Krasnoyarsk Territory and the Koryak Area in Kamchatka that have already claimed their rights.

Special privileges granted to subjects of the Russian Federation furnish them a large degree of economic autonomy. The republics are entitled to establish their national banks (due agreements have been concluded with 20 republics of the Russian Federation); according to the Russian Ministry of Justice, a special provision in the unpublished Annex to the Federative Treaty makes the republican courts the highest instance in legal procedures; land and natural resources are taken out of control of the center; and certain regions like Sakhalin are not obliged to comply to the all-Russian investment law.

In summer and fall 1992 the process of regionalization gained momentum. The Koryak Autonomous Area proclaimed its secession from Kamchatka, discussions continued concerning the establishment of the Far Eastern Republic, the Omsk Oblast decided to sell tanks on its own. Also there was proof that the Ukranian government had been trying to facilitate the weakening of the central authority in Russia (Ukraine has signed an economic and political agreement with the Tyumen Oblast, a sort of "diplomatic relation" was established between the Chernigov Oblast of Ukraine and the Yaroslavl Oblast of Russia, etc.). The August 1992 decision of Moscow to abolish the system of centralized distribution of natural resources also led to the dissolution of economic authority in Russia.

The regionalization of Russia is facilitated by a visible usurpation of authority in the localities. The functions of the state power are assumed by local political, social, ethnic, and sometimes even criminal groups. It is bluntly demonstrated by the evolution of the politically oriented Cossack movement that has finally become an issue of general politics, by the armament of Cossacks who assume the rights of law enforcement bodies, and by unwarranted participation of Cossacks in military conflicts beyond the borders of Russia (in Pridnestrovye, North Caucasus), discrediting the foreign policy and peacemaking efforts of Moscow.

The regionalization of Russia develops in an uneven manner. More inclined to economic and political separatism are regions with a high rate of raw materials and the territories with a higher degree of economic self-sufficiency (i.e. those that can allegedly maintain themselves and produce marketable goods for barter trade). Such are, for example, some southern regions of Russia like Lipetsk and Belgorod Oblasts, Krasnodar and Stavropol Territories, etc. Oblasts with less potential for sustaining themselves (like the Yaroslavl Oblast) and the so-called "subsidized" Oblasts (the Magadan Oblast) are more dependent on the center and have less possibilities for political maneuver.

Regionalization Policies by the Russian Government

Assessing the prospects for the dissolution (or even a radical break-up) of Russia, one should not miss the subjective factor, i.e. the ability of the central power to keep the situation under control. The first year of actual independence gave enough proof of inconsistency and hesitation of the leadership of Russia in its approach to the possible breakup of the country. Absolutely lacking was a special policy that would render movements and forces threatening the territorial integrity of the state illegitimate. This was well demonstrated by President Yeltsin's contradictory statements on the creation of the German autonomous region during 1991–1992, by complete failure of imposing the state of emergency in the Chechen Republic in fall 1991, by conflicting and irresponsible promises of Moscow concerning the Prigorodny District in Vladikavkaz (both contesting parties, Ingushis and Osetians, were promised the same territory), that finally resulted in a military conflict in October 1992.

The efforts to pursue a federative and regional policy have practically no legal grounds or guarantees. Beside evident facts, like the absence of a Constitution of the Russian Federation and the amorphous and non-abiding character of the Federative Treaty, there is no distinct division of competence and power, as exemplified by unclear and concurring positions of new people on the Russian political scene: the heads of local administrations and the local representatives of the President. As a result, they are usually incorporated into local establishments. Such a lack of regional politics and of legal provisions may be seen as a gradual transfer of authority from the center to the regions.

Most probably the process of disintegration in Russia will widen and deepen. In theory, provided the current trends continue, the regionalization could proceed until it finally determines all economic subjects that will be able to take possession of the former state property, or, in case of economic collapse, until the optimum-sized economic and territorial units that will prove most viable are developed. Also possible is the contrary process of reintegration of some adjacent Oblasts and Autonomous Republics into major regions with the purpose of a more effective struggle with the center (in the same way the national democratic movements united to oppose Gorbachev's center in late perestroika years). The regional coalitions are already being established, like the Association of Oblasts of Central Russia, the "Greater Volga" Association, the Confederation of the Mountaineer Nations of the Caucasus with armed forces of its own, the elementary bodies of the Far Eastern Republic, etc. In any case, the regionalization will result in the rise and self-determination of economic and political subjects that are now still in a shapeless state.

The consequences of regionalization may be of two kinds. On one side, the decay of the imperial body of Russia may result in the dramatic increase of ethnic, inter-regional or even inter-oblast contradictions, in "Balkanization" or "Lebanonization" of Russia and the entire territory of the former Soviet Union. Thus the regionalization of the state is fraught with the following sorts of conflicts:
1. The ethnic conflict on the periphery (Chechnya, Daghestan, the Adigei Region, Karachayevo, etc.).
2. Conflicts in republics with balanced ethnic composition that seek to create a monoethnic elite and a monoethnic regime (Tatarstan, Bashkortostan, Chuvashia).
3. The economic conflict in a monoethnic regions supplying raw materials that primarily concerns their control over resources and their share in profit from sales (Tyumen, Chita, the Kuznetsk coal basin, Karelia).
4. The conflict of large cities with regions supplying agricultural production and raw materials (like the "blockade of Moscow" in Fall 1991).
5. The social conflict in an industrial center struck by crises, layoffs, unemployment, etc. (like in the Ural).
6. The political conflict resulting from the struggle among local elites.
7. Regionalization on the verge of political disintegration. In this case the armed forces will most probably be moved in (or will move in), to prevent that development. This will result in an establishment of a more authoritarian regime, or, if such a move fails, in quickening Lebanonization.

On the other hand, the regionalization could as well contribute to the social, economic and political stability. The regions can become that long-awaited "third force" (given the "first force" is the government that finds itself in growing isolation from actual developments and does not possess effective mechanisms of power, and the "second" is the opposition that insists on the straightforward and rather unpopular idea of integration) that will be able to fill the power vacuum and slow the conflict-bearing trends.

The foundations are already being laid for the creation of regional parties lobbying in the center (this is encouraged by an unprecedented corruption in high echelons of power) and impacting the state policy. This trend gains momentum, as exemplified by the prominent Russian politician Nicolai Travkin, one of the leaders of the "Civic Union". He consolidates a political base not only on the national, but also on the regional level, by taking charge of the Shakhovskoy District in the Moscow Oblast.

Thus the regionalization of Russia does not inevitably lead to a Balkanization, and may take a rather peaceful and productive course. One can envisage the following alternatives:
- full political isolation of regions that does not necessarily mean the break of all economic ties. The regions will simply emerge as self-confident political and economic subjects and will act accordingly;
- a "soft" federation in which the regions form the central authority with the role of an inter-regional economic committee, and cede a small part of their rights to it; most foreign and defense policies are conducted from Moscow, while foreign economic policies are pursued by the regions within one general framework;
- a "two-speed" variant, in which the center manages nation-wide affairs (security, foreign policy, etc.), and the regions are in charge of the economy;
- a flexible association with several levels of participation, in which part of the regions enter into a federation with the center (Oblasts of the Central, North-Eastern Russia, the Ural, etc.), some choose a confederation (Yakut-Sakha, Komi, Bashkortostan), and some, like Tatarstan, will become associate members.

In any case, there are many alternatives, and some may look relatively appealing. The disintegration of Russia does not only pose questions but also offers some kinds of answers.

There is no immediate threat of a political disintegration of Russia. However, the weakness of the state structures and the absence of a coherent policy on disintegration/decentralization could bring about a situation of a different quality, when the process of disintegration will really start. The actual course of events will become clearer during 1993–1994.

2. Ethno-Political Conflicts on the Territory of the Former USSR

Motives

Ethnic conflicts on the territory of the former Soviet Union have emerged as a main factor of destabilization in Russia and the CIS, and the most critical threat to peace and international order. Like other multinational states of Eastern Europe – Yugoslavia, Rumania and Czechoslovakia – the former USSR undergoes a dangerous phase of state construction among hitherto stateless nations that were subject to unitarian authority.

The process of national self-government generally outpaces the restructuring of economic, political and judicial institutions of the society, and is usually accompanied by the search for a national self-consciousness which deems "the right of the nation" superior over the rights of the individual. All this is fraught with the emergence and the escalation of conflicts.

There are multiple conflict-bearing factors on the territory of the former Soviet Union, including:
- the dissolution of the political power, the decomposition of the state structures and the society itself on all levels, the psychological atmosphere of decay and destruction;
- the new ambitions of the local elites and the centers of power to achieve autonomy, provoked by the breakup of the corporate Soviet power structure; the struggle for consolidation within the elites; the struggle of the competing elites for local and regional power; the opposition of the local elites to the new republican centers;
- the new tactic of the local communist and nomenklatura forces aimed at forming an alliance with nationalist movements or preserving the regime by proclaiming sovereignty;
- consolidation of the pro-imperial forces;
- lack of conflict strategies and mere incompetence of most actors

on the post-Soviet political scene.
This is further complicated by the intricate ethnic and demographic situation. There are over 150 nations on the territory of the former Soviet Union, most of which have their "own" territories of compact residence, over 70 million people (including some 28 million Russians) live outside their native regions, and there are about 13 million "mixed" inter-ethnic families (nearly 50 million people).

Fundamental Conditions of the Ethno-Cultural Escalation

Ethno-political conflicts on the territory of the former Soviet Union, the dramatic escalation of which started in about 1989 (it had been only Nagorny Karabakh before, where the major armed conflict was taking place), can be divided into several main types:
1. **Riots and pogroms.** There were the pogroms of Meskheti Turks in Ferghana (Uzbekistan) in 1989, of Uzbeks in Osh (Kirghizstan) and of Armenians in Dushanbe (Tajikistan) in 1990, and a number of other conflicts that are generally euphemistically called "events". Hidden behind each of them is a specific political interest that turns the outrage of the mob against a non-native ethnic group which becomes a scapegoat. For instance, standing behind the pogroms of Meskheti Turks in Ferghana were the interests of the Kokand political elite that was willing to show the new authorities of Tashkent the limits of their influence in the Ferghana region.
The conflicts of such type can be triggered by demographic and economic problems, especially by unemployment. It is not by mere chance that all of the conflicts mentioned above took place in regions with a high percentage of a non-working population. Most risky is the situation in large cities with a multinational population, particularly in lumpen districts. Repeated disturbances in the cities of Central Russia aimed at visitors from the Caucasus testify to the rise of social and racial strife. The capitals are no exception. The racial conflict in Moscow in August 1992 involving students from the Third World is an exotic, but still a telling example.
In case of a sharp aggravation of the social and economic crisis riots and pogroms can be taking place anywhere, though most explosive will be the places with a high concentration of refugees.
2. **A conflict between the native ethnic group and the non-native population on the territories that have obtained full or partial independence.** The conflict is focussed mainly on the rights of the non-native (mostly Russian-speaking) population. The new independent

states and sovereign Autonomous Republics (the Baltic states, Moldova, some Autonomous Republics of Russia) are living through a period of violent assertion of their national statehood that often takes place at the cost of civil rights of the heteroethnic population, and is accompanied by a discriminatory ethnic-biased legislation. This tendency has also appeared in Central Asia and Kazakhstan, but fortunately is dormant in Ukraine. Given the fact that Moscow does not have any strategy of protection of the Russian-speaking population in the neighboring states, and given its contradictory actions ranging from military involvement to mere neglect of the compatriots, conflicts of this kind can be spreading quickly.

3. **A conflict as a delayed consequence of Stalinist deportations of entire nations in 1937-1941.** Such conflicts appear in places where these nations were forced to settle (as in the mentioned case of the Meskheti pogroms in Ferghana), as well as on their return to the native land. The latter is exemplified by the conflict between the Crimean Tartars coming back to the Crimea, and the Slavic population of the peninsula.

4. **An open armed conflict between local political elites within one republic.** Such conflicts become characteristic of a growing number of former Soviet republics: Armenia, Georgia, Azerbaijan, Tajikistan... A typical case is Georgia where a four-year conflict continues between the West Georgian, particularly Menghrelian, political elite personified by the ex-president Zviad Gamsakhurdia, and the Tbilisi political establishment currently represented by Edouard Shevardnadze, Tengiz Kitovani and Djaba Ioseliani. A dramatic conflict of this kind is currently taking place in Tajikistan.

5. **A conflict concerning the status of the ethnic territory** (i.e. a dispute about upgrading the status of the territory – from cultural to administrative autonomy, and up to self-government and separation as a state). Conflicts of this kind are widely spread across the territory of the former USSR: South Osetia, Abkhazia, Pridnestrovye, Gagauzia, Chechnya, Tatarstan. They are closely connected with emerging imperial trends of the new republican regimes, including the ambitions of some (Georgia) to become a regional gendarme.

6. **A conflict concerning disputed territories that each of the conflicting parties considers a part of its historical homeland.** A typical example of such a conflict is the dispute between Inghushis and Osetians over the Prigorodny District of Vladikavkaz. The conflict in Nagorny Karabakh originated exactly in such a form.

7. **An interstate conflict.** Currently there is a single interstate military conflict taking place between Armenia and Azerbaijan. It is actu-

ally a war going on at three fronts: in Nagorny Karabakh itself (this is an enclave with an Armenian majority on the Azeri territory), along the Armenian-Azeri border, and on the border between Armenia and Nakhichevan, Azeri territory separated from the mainland.

Another instance of escalation of an interstate conflict is the crisis in the Russian-Ukranian relations concerning security, and diplomatic, and economic fields. There are a number of latent conflict pairs of the kind, like Russia and Kazakhstan, Kazakhstan and Uzbekistan, Belarus and Lithuania, Russia and Estonia, Moldova and Ukraine.

Functions of the Ethno-Regional Conflicts

With the breakup of the centralized power structure of the former USSR and the dissolution of the single political space, ethno-political conflicts have taken on various functions. Their most important role, as mentioned, is that they serve to determine real subjects of political power and the true balance of forces on the territory of the former Soviet Union. The other functions include:

1. **Conflict as a means in the struggle for power**, often used by the opposition. This is shown by the regulated interstate conflict between Armenia and Azerbaijan that has actually brought to power the present leaders of these Transcaucasian states. The current Azeri president Abulfaz Elchibei replaced his predecessor Ayaz Mutalibov at the peak of public discontent with defeats in Karabakh. As to the Armenian president Levon Ter-Petrosyan, he came to office with the 'Karabakh Committee', and represents a specific 'Karabakh layer' in the Yerevan political establishment.
2. **Conflict as a means to hold power.** This is clearly exemplified by the political continuity of the Tbilisi regime from Zviad Gamsakhurdia to Edouard Shevardnadze. Both leaders were vitally interested in the "war of attrition" in South Osetia as a means of consolidating the nation and strengthening the regime. Since that conflict was scaling down, Shevardnadze shifted the cross hairs of confrontation on Sukhumi. The war in Abkhazia enabled Shevardnadze to legitimize his power and to appear as the "defender of the nation" on the eve of the parliamentary elections that he won by a landslide.

In Moldova the president Mircia Sneghur has repeatedly encouraged confrontation in Pridnestrovye in order to appear more nationalist-minded than the opposition. For instance, the opposition was planning a nation-wide meeting on March 29, 1992, that is the anniversary of the unification of Bessarabia, where it was going to demand the resignation of the president. Sneghur cast a preventive blow, and on March 28, precisely on the eve of the meeting, declared a state of emergency in Pridnestrovye.

General Djohar Dudayev in the Chechen Republic acts very much the same, pursuing the politics of regulated conflict with Moscow with the purpose of consolidating the nation and the ruling elite, and above all – his hold on power.

The most obvious example is the course of the Ukrainian government, for which the policies of controlled tension with Moscow is one of the main instruments of state building.

3. **Conflict as means of geopolitical pressure.** It is primarily Russia that can use regional conflicts with this purpose, but also Ukraine, and some countries adjacent to the CIS, like Poland, Rumania, Turkey, Iran, Afghanistan, China, and Japan. Until present, the politics of the Kremlin has not given evidence to such an approach. Given the spontaneous character of Boris Yeltsin's statements, the practical politics of the President and the government never went beyond the limits the world community could call aggressive. The potential for such politics, however, exists, as exemplified by imperial impulses in the Moscow political establishment. A number of regional conflicts (state of emergency in Chechnya, wars in Pridnestrovye and Abkhazia, etc.) were used for consolidating pro-imperial elements within Russia.

Impacts

Each ethno-political conflict on the former Soviet territory spreads in a horizontal and vertical direction. Firstly, it widens in space, provoking the neighboring states to conflict behavior. Thus the Abkhaz crisis of Summer and Fall 1992 has increased tensions in the entire North Caucasus, on the Stavropol Territory, and aroused a sharp reaction of the leadership of Bashkortostan. Secondly, the conflict deepens in the social, political and economic life, resulting in further disintegration on all levels. It has a deep impact, including:
- **political consequences**: the decay of the legislative, executive and judicial powers, the distortion of the public legal consciousness, the devaluation of law and traditional morals, the strengthening of authoritarian trends in politics, the suppression of democracy, and the possible emergence of fascist leaders;
- **economic consequences**: plain destruction, the stoppage of produc-

tion, the disturbance of the production cycle of cooperating enterprises, the fall of the business activity, the breakup of economic ties, the devastation of the already weak economies by one-sided militarization;
- **environmental consequences**: the general weakening of environmental security, the possibility of a nuclear and chemical contamination, planned actions aimed at the destruction of the ecosystem (demolition of dams, setting on fire oil reservoirs and forests, contamination of rivers and subsoil waters, etc.);
- **demographic and social consequences**: the danger of extermination of entire ethnic groups, the disturbance of the natural reproduction, the forced migration of the population, the refugee problem and shifts in the demographic structure, the aggravation of food and housing problems, unemployment;
- **psychological consequences**: the spread of armed violence as a common lifestyle.

Quite as present is the danger of ethno-political conflicts in the former USSR for the outer world. The threat of nuclear terrorism is still feasible. Masses of refugees from conflict zones will bring permanent pressure on Europe even under the most strict immigration regime. There is a risk of mass terrorism spreading over the limits of the former USSR and East Europe. A desperate social and psychological atmosphere in the areas of ethnic conflicts may yield terrorism akin to fanaticism of Irish, Palestinian or Tamil militants. Taken in general, expansion of conflict zones on the territory of the former Soviet Union may lead to the emergence of a vast area of permanent instability that will be spreading to neighboring regions and all over the world.

With the emergence of such an enormous "pot of instability" on the eastern frontiers of Europe, the West will be facing a hard security dilemma: either the risk that the flows of chaos and decay will splash out on Europe, on still fragile integration mechanisms – or the erection of a new "iron curtain", isolation of the explosive region, that, given the growing global interdependence, will most likely prove futile or even counterproductive.

The international community, however, has the third choice: an attempt to facilitate transition in the former Soviet Union. This is a special topic that can not be treated in detail in this report, and demands a special research. However, one remark has to be made. The politics of international engagement will also be facing special problems – and most notably, the generally recognized principle of non-interference in the internal affairs of other countries. As far as the subject of foreign politics on the territory of the former USSR will be splitting into smaller units, the international community, pulling "inside" the specific conflict, will be inevitably facing the protest of a more or less legitimate state entity. This makes any international involvement a more challenging problem to tackle, but does not mean the impossibility of international participation in managing and resolving ethno-political conflicts on the territory of the former USSR, that pose the most serious danger to the international peace.

3. Economic Space of the Former USSR and the Prospects for Market Reforms

Economical Frame

The Commonwealth of Independent States has been established by former Soviet republics which accounted for the main part of the Soviet economic potential. Their share in the total of the USSR was in terms of territory 1990 – 98 percent population – 97 percent national income, industrial production – 94 percent foreign trade – 93 percent agricultural production – 92. (see *table 1*).

The CIS was joined by all of the five former biggest Soviet republics: The Russian Federation, or Russia – a giant among them (*table 1*), with a major part of Soviet natural resources being located on its soil; Ukraine has 16 percent of the Soviet national income; Belarus 4 percent; Kazakhstan 4 percent, Uzbekistan 3 percent correspondingly.

The CIS members are still characterized by a high economic interdependence. The inter-republican exchange in 1990 made up more than one fifth of the USSR national product. It exceeded by more than two times the Soviet exports to the outside world. A major part of inter-republican exchanges were "tied up" on Russia, which played a leading role in this sphere as well. Russia supplied other republics with raw oil products, natural gas, timber, some other commodities and received from them agricultural products and industrial consumption goods. There was also a deep intra-republican division of labor in machine-building and other branches of manufacturing, which included millions of separate positions.

After the dissolution of the USSR all new independent states proclaimed their intentions, although with a different degree of conviction, to continue the policy of democratization and transformation to a market economy, started during the perestroika years. This formed a suitable political basis for a continued economic cooperation among CIS member countries.

Finally, all successor states of the USSR inherited from the Soviet period a deep economic crises (*table 2*).

Russia, Ukraine, Moldova, Kazakhstan, Tajikistan, Armenia suffered the deepest decline of industrial and agricultural production. Shortages of food and other consumption goods reached intolerable dimensions. An uncontrolled price rise started. Foreign trade virtually collapsed. Foreign indebtedness increased to an unprecedented level. The urgency of economic stabilization requested from all the CIS countries not only a continuation, but a broadening of their economic cooperation.

While establishing the CIS, its member countries decided to coordinate their economic policies in such important questions as "carrying out radical economic reforms directed at the creation of full-fledged market mechanisms, transformation of ownership relations, promotion of free enterprise". They agreed also to safeguard "by common efforts" "the unity of economic space" and "not to allow a downturn of mutual economic exchanges". But no special bodies for an economic cooperation and no control procedure for the fulfillment of agreements have been established at the CIS level. The realization of declared intentions met in practice with great difficulties as well.

Kazakhstan, Belarus, Kirghizstan, and Russia showed readiness to coordinate their economic development, to preserve the common economic space, and to intrust the CIS with effective functions.

Contrary to that, Ukraine decided to establish its economic independence, to introduce its own currency ("*grivna*"), and to restrict its cooperation with CIS to an interstate level only. A policy of a passive participation in CIS economic activities was also selected by Turkmenistan.

A situation full of contradictions developed in the rouble zone. The newly established national (central) banks in CIS countries started their own rouble credit emissions without any coordination with the Russian Central Bank. It became an important source of inflation in Russia, undermining its efforts to stabilize the rouble. Credit emissions by Ukraine got especially big dimensions.

"Coupons" as a surrogate of the rouble had been introduced by Ukraine as a first step towards its own national currency, and by Belarus, Moldova, Azerbaijan to compensate for a deficit of cash which was inflicted at the beginning of 1992 on all CIS countries.

A change from "intrarepublican" to interstate relationships requested a new approach to price setting in mutual trade almost immediately. Russia started to accumulate significant trade surpluses resulting mainly from the rise in energy prices, which had been kept in the former Soviet Union at an artificially low level. There was also a general big growth of prices in intra-CIS exchanges. World market prices or prices close to them gradually began to substitute former common internal wholesale prices.

Turkmenistan, an important supplier of natural gas, stopped gas deliveries to Ukraine which insisted on maintaining the old low Soviet wholesale price for this commodity, at the beginning of 1992.

Differences arose also from an approach to market reforms. The policy of Russia got a special importance for the economic development of all CIS countries.

Russias Economical Reform Therapy

At the beginning of 1992 Russia started a radical market reform. A model of monetary "shock therapy" was selected. It included a liberalization of prices (with the exception of prices for energy and fuels which were raised but remained under state control), and restrictive monetary and credit policy (a reduction of budgetary expenditures on defense, capital investments and some other purposes; an increase of taxes and credit rates and a restriction of emissions).

Privatization was started in internal trade, services, construction and some other branches. In agriculture measures to promote the establishment of private farms and to dissolve or reorganize ineffective collective and state farms were introduced.

Foreign economic relations have been liberalized. Russia joined the International Monetary Fund (IMF) and the International Bank for Reconstruction and Development (IBRD) and took over the USSR seat at the European Bank for Reconstruction and Development (EBRD). It concluded a preliminary stand-by agreement with the IMF.

Reforms started in Russia under difficult conditions. The economy lost its manageability. Changes met with political resistance in the Supreme Soviet, which was not re-elected after the gain of independence by Russia. Separatist trends increased in several autonomous republics (Tatarstan and Chechnya) and in some other regions.

However, even in these difficult circumstances by fall 1992 first positive results of the reform became visible. A price environment was created as the main condition under which a market economy can function. 90 percent of the production was already carried out in a free price environment. Lines at shops nearly disappeared. Money became a most desired commodity.

The role of private commercial structures in production and especially in trade increased. The population showed a high degree of adaptability to new conditions.

Germany, the European Communities, the United States, and other Western countries granted Russia humanitarian, technical and some financial assistance. Debts have been rescheduled.

In agriculture, too, certain progress was achieved. The number of private farms grew from 45 to 135 thousand and the area of their lands expanded from 2.1 to 5.6 million of hectares during the first eight month of 1992. More than 6000 collective and state farms were radically transformed or dissolved.

At the same time, the general economic situation did not improve and in many instances even worsened considerably. There was a further deep decline of industrial and agricultural production. Inflation became rampant. The indebtedness of enterprises reached enormous dimensions. The very existence of a number of the most important and technologically most modern branches of industry was endangered. The financial situation in agriculture became critical. The exchange rate of the rouble collapsed.

Despite a rise of wages and salaries, pensions and other social allocations, the standard of living went down strikingly. The number of reform opponents increased.

In 1992 other CIS countries, and first of all Kazakhstan, Belarus, Kirghizstan, Armenia, and Ukraine also began to introduce market reforms, but at a slower pace. In certain cases, as for example in the liberalization of prices, they were obliged to follow the more decisive Russian actions.

Like Russia, all of them suffered a further downturn of output, and a growth of the indebtedness of the enterprises. Everywhere prices soared.

In mid-1992 the government of Russia announced the entry of economic reforms into the second stage. "The program of the deepening of economic reforms" intended for 2–3 years was presented to the Supreme Soviet for consideration. Influential political movements and parties put forward their own alternative programs. The discussion has not been completed. It seems, however, that the market reforms in Russia will be continued in any case. They are not objected in principle even by the majority of opposing forces. They have the support of the main part of the population despite the declining living standard. At the same time it is obvious that the strategy of reforms will undergo considerable corrections. An acceleration of the privatization may be put in the forefront.

The transforming of large-scale enterprises (6–7 thousand) into joint-stock companies could be completed in 1992–1993. In 1993 35 percent of their shares amounting to about 1.5 trillion roubles (1991 prices) are to be exchanged for vouchers (privatization cheques handed out to all Russian citizens). The hope is to create a many-million class of proprietors which will become a social basis for further motion to the market. The other aim is to convert the directors of the state-owned enterprises – the most influential strata of the elite – into owners of their enterprises, thus changing their interests and bringing them into the camp of supporters of a continuation of further capitalist and eventually democratic reforms. In 1995 the share of the privatized property in large-scale industry may reach 50–60 percent.

It would mean a change of Russia from a "socialist" state with dominant state ownership to a country with a diversified property including its state, private and corporative forms and guided mainly by market forces.

In agriculture free development and co-existence of private farming and efficient collective and state farms will be pursued.

The speeding-up of economic stabilization and an intensified promotion of structural change should become another new direction of reforms. It will include different market and budgetary measures to support the basic industries (fuel and energies, food, housing construction, and communications), to speed up the conversion of the military sector to civilian purposes and to save those branches which are the carriers of scientific and technical progress. Light industries may also get additional attention.

A strict monetary and budgetary policy, a struggle against inflation will remain an important direction of reforms in Russia. But the contradiction will sharpen between requirements to constrain budgetary expenditures, investments, credits, emission, and to find additional means for financing structural changes and safeguarding the living standard of the population. It will be one of the most difficult problems in the relations of Russia with the IMF.

As far as the prospects of economic stabilization are concerned, it can be expected that in 1993 the downturn of the production will continue, but the pace of the decline may decelerate. In 1994–1995 the output may stabilize. After 1995–1997 a resumption of growth could become possible.

Russia: Model for the CIS

In the years to come an acceleration of reforms may be expected in majority of other CIS countries, notably in Kazakhstan, Belarus and

Kirghizstan. In Ukraine in October 1992 a government which procrastinated was obliged to resign. Turkmenistan may be a certain exception, although the situation in this country is yet not quite clear.

One may suppose that while there is a considerable variety of specific situations in separate countries of the CIS, the dynamics of their economic development in the nearest future will be largely following that of Russia. It is evident that in all these countries the decline in production in 1993 will go on. It will be more profound in zones of military conflicts. The dynamics of the production in Ukraine may be adversely affected by its course for self-isolation from the CIS countries (should it be continued), at least in short-term. Under these circumstances the absense of economic policies and major exportable natural resources brought about a fall of production, which is much deeper than in Russia and most countries of the former USSR. Ukraine received about $2 billion in credit pledges from the outside world. But their possible use will hardly change the general difficult economic situation in this country.

Since the formation of the CIS there have been some important changes in economic relations among its member states. Sovereignty of partners got recognition and a new legal framework for interstate relations began to be established in the form of different bilateral agreements on trade and economic cooperation.

Russia has signed agreements on trade and economic cooperation in 1992 with all interested CIS states. It concluded also a range of much broader agreements with Belarus, Kazakhstan, Kirghizstan, and some other members of the CIS. They provided for a free movement of goods, services, capital and people and for maintenance of the common economic space.

The organizational structure of former intra-republican deliveries showed some new features. Partner states guaranteed the supply of agreed quantities of some of the most important commodities by administrative measures and in certain cases at fixed prices. But a growing share of turnover already resulted from normal commercial deals between enterprises of cooperating countries.

Relations with Ukraine were improved. After a period of sharp contradictions at the beginning of the year, in May 1992 a Russian-Ukrainian agreement on the development of interstate relations was signed. It proclaimed, at least in words, the establishment of a partner relationship between two countries. An intermediate solution for the Black Sea fleet was found. The use of world market prices in mutual relations and measures to be taken in connection with the introduction of its own currency by Ukraine were agreed on. At a later stage such questions as the growth of Ukrainian indebtedness to Russia, uncontrolled rouble credit emissions by the Ukrainian National Bank, transit of Russian natural gas to Europe through Ukrainian territory came to a partial solution.

However, divergences of views on a number of questions of mutual relations continued to exist. In October 1992 Ukraine decided once more to postpone the change to *grivna*. But for internal clearing purposes a new rouble ("*karbovanetz*") was to be introduced from the beginning of 1993. Ukraine has settled its dispute with Turkmenistan, having agreed to buy Turkmenian natural gas at prices close to the world level.

Bilateral relations will remain the basis for economic cooperation among CIS member-states in the future as well. In fall 1992 Russia reached agreements on trade and economic cooperation in 1993 with all its main CIS partners. It also signed new agreements with a number of CIS states (Armenia, Kirghizstan, Tajikistan, some other) on the maintenance of a common economic space, free trade, cooperation in transportation and transit questions and so on. It also has to be noted that bilateral agreements have been concluded on a common monetary system and a coordinated monetary, credit and foreign currency policy. That could eventually end the uncertainty which prevailed in the rouble zone, as has been noted above.

The New Kind of Intra-Cooperation Forms of the CIS

Economic cooperation in the framework of CIS began to develop on a multilateral basis as well. Agreements were signed by member states concerning the conservation of a single system of railways, scientific-technical collaboration; on an agreed policy of standardization, metrology and certification; concerning guarantees of the rights of citizens to get a pension. Beside this, agreements were reached on such fundamental questions as the principles of a unification of the economic legislation of member states; mutual recognition of rights and regulation of ownership relations and customs policy. A multilateral agreement on "a single monetary system and agreed credit and monetary policy of the states, which maintained the rouble as a legal means of payment" is also to be noted. It supplemented bilateral agreements mentioned above and strengthened the basis for a new contractual relationship among rouble zone participants.

Some multilateral bodies to promote economic cooperation have been created. They included an economic court of the CIS to resolve economic disputes among member countries an interbank coordination council of the national (central) banks of the states of the rouble area, a consultative economic commission, and the interstate bank for settling payments among CIS member countries. But they have yet to start functioning and to show their efficiency.

The major part of the multilateral agreements mentioned above have not been signed by Ukraine and Turkmenistan and in certain cases by Moldova. But they are not directed against non-signatures and may be joined by them at a later stage.

Regardless of some progress, it seems that the activity of the CIS in the economic domain does not correspond fully to the task to stabilize and to develop mutual economic exchange among member countries. It has no stable legal basis, does not cover a number of important matters which were agreed upon while creating the Commonwealth (e.g. the coordination of market reforms). However gradually, this activity is widening.

It can be assumed that in the future there will be a further growth of interest in CIS countries towards a better use of CIS potential for the development of a mutual cooperation on a multilateral basis.

It also seems probable that the trend towards the development of a cooperation in the framework of CIS among member countries "at different speed" would strengthen. This implies the creation of an integration nucleus, consisting of Russia, Belarus, Kazakhstan, maybe Uzbekistan and possibly (at a later stage) of some other states, and a broad and diversified cooperation among them and other member-countries (notably Ukraine and Turkmenistan) on a regular interstate basis. However, the situation will remain unstable, and a possibility of changes in membership of both groups can not be excluded.

Alongside with a stabilization of the economic and political situation in the CIS states, the search by this group of countries for new methods of promoting and organizing their economic relations with the outside world may be intensified.

4. The Military and Political Aspects

The abortive military coup in August 1991 set about the process that eventually led to the collapse of the USSR and the formation of the CIS in December 1991. Relative success of its latest summit meetings and the emerging centripetal trends within the Commonwealth indicate that the CIS, which looked frail and impotent in its cradle, will in this or that shape rumble on for the foreseeable future. It means among other things, that its evolving military security setup will be in place for the years to come.

As Russia under no realistic circumstances quits the CIS, its military security will be linked to that of the CIS and its members. It is also reasonable to assume, that for years and even decades Russia is highly unlikely to abandon its newly acquired military and political identity, even if the CIS moves towards becoming a loose confederation – or a tighter federation – of states. So for conceptual as well as practical reasons it is advisable to discuss in parallel the likely ways of military evolution by Russia and the CIS.

Carrying on with the CIS

Very few words have been said about **reasons behind the existence of the CIS,** and especially its **military justification**. An analysis indicates, that there are at least five security objectives which the Commonwealth is to solve in the future:
a. To facilitate and make less dangerous the process of adopting unique military identities by each of the former Soviet republics comprising the CIS.
b. To enhance the security of individual republics, since most of them are unable to establish a reliable defense on their own.
c. To prevent ethnic, religious, and economic conflicts and border disputes within the former Soviet Union or at least to contain and help solve them.

d. To save money by organizing a "joint security venture".

e. To present some kind of collective military credibility to the outside world, as its military force still has some reputation at present.

It is very doubtful that the CIS will fully live up to these demands. It has already stumbled on the first point being unable to prevent a confrontation between Russia and Ukraine over the division of authority over the strategic forces on the Ukrainian territory and the Black Sea fleet. The Commonwealth will be of little help in settling similar disputes in the future. It is indicative, that the Black Sea fleet issue was finally removed from the CIS agenda and transformed into a purely bilateral one. The only consolation is that there are few remaining issues here. One of them is to secure the speediest and safest transition of Ukraine, Belarus and Kazakhstan to a non-nuclear status and to divide rights and obligations between Russia and the Central Asian republics in the south of the former Soviet Union.

The CIS may be of some real help in improving military security of its members with a view to the outside world. The main immediate beneficiary here will be Russia which hopes to retain the present layer of friendly and neutral buffer zones around its periphery. But Russia probably cannot wholeheartedly reckon upon other republics' help in time of a hypothetical military crisis, because some of them may be politically unwilling to come to rescue (like Ukraine), while others will lack sufficient military resources to significantly relieve Russia's plight.

Other republics are less keen about immediate protection from an outside military intervention because today they do not see hostile nations beyond their "outer borders". But with a view to the future they are still interested in some form of common defense: while immediate danger is not present, it may be materialized as the result of multiple potential border and territorial disputes (Belarus-Poland, Ukraine-Rumania, and Kazakhstan-China).

For all the CIS states the chief aim of the Commonwealth at present and for years to come is to prevent or at least to help settle intra-CIS disputes, the internal strive and conflicts in any of its member states. The problem is that the collapse of the Soviet Union had brought multiple internal tensions in many of its regions into the open. These tensions have subsequently turned into armed confrontations. Such conflicts have been made much more intensive and deadly due to the dubious decision taken by the Russian leaders on sharing out the military assets of the former Soviet Union. Such assets were largely under Russia's control and it was up to Russia to determine what to do with them. Moscow opted for a short-sighted policy, containing two major elements. Firstly, it agreed on specific and rather high weapons ceilings for the republics who had entered the CFE process. Secondly, Moscow voluntarily decided to hand over light and heavy lethal military equipment to the politically opposed and even belligerent sides. It was like pouring oil into the fire. Unfortunately, it will be very difficult for the Russian leadership to stop the inertia of that move and switch over to clear-cut rebuttals of the still coming claims to the russian controlled weapons and equipment in the CIS trouble spots.

So, the CIS and its members being crisis-prone and conflict-ridden are in dire need for some mechanism to put the situation right.

Unfortunately, the CIS' record here is not very impressive. So far the Commonwealth has admittedly failed to quell or mediate in conflicts between its members Azerbaijan and Armenia, and inside Moldova and Tajikistan. The best judgment is that the CIS will most likely continue in this way in the short and medium-term perspective. The only clear-cut positive example was putting down the Ossetian conflict.

To be in the position to authoritatively intervene in such dispute, the CIS must first of all have a high standing with its participants, political will, and a legal basis for such an intervention, all of which are lacking. They are unlikely to emerge soon, given the diversity of views and positions within the Commonwealth.

The best the CIS as a collective body may hope to achieve in the field of peace-making in this decade is to act as fire-extinguisher, putting an end to the most bitter armed conflicts. It looks improbable that the Commonwealth will ever have "medicine" to cure root causes of internal and intra-CIS disputes. But even this limited role will be of utmost importance to the safety and stability of the CIS members and its close and more distant neighbors.

There are at least two unpleasant consequences to such an assessment of the CIS as a peace-maker. Firstly, pacifying conflicts within the CIS will call for foreign (CSCE, UN) involvement or individual actions by one or more "senior" CIS members (notably Russia) offering its good offices. Secondly, Russia will find itself in the most unenviable position. As Russia is the "senior" member of the CIS it cannot really expect any help from the Commonwealth in solving its internal problems of disintegration.

The CIS is an unreliable mechanism to save "defense money", at least as far as the bigger republics are concerned. The three Slavic republics are sure to go their own ways appropriating as much money for defense as they could afford (not much). The same is true for the quarrelling Caucasian nations. The Central Asian republics do not have much financial and material resources to invest in their own defense establishments (and to create something better than national guards) or in collective security.

Finally, the CIS, ridden by uncertainty, lack of internal unity and clear-cut military guidance can hardly be taken as a formidable force to be reckoned with, compared to the now defunct Soviet Union. However, some of its individual members may be considered in military terms as regional powers, and Russia may rely on its nuclear arsenal to establish its global credentials.

In other words, the CIS will play a rather limited but still important role. The second issue for discussion **is the role of individual states within the CIS security framework** in the short- to medium term perspective (more distant developments – beyond the year 2000 – are impossible to predict due to a very volatile situation in practically all of the republics).

The CIS has entered a period of relative stability with no upheavals in the offing. But this does not exclude its evolution, prompted among other things by constant fluctuations in the republics' attitudes towards security-related CIS treaties and formal obligations stemming from them, i.e. by the varying levels of political and military integration ("the degree of affiliation") of member states in the CIS now and in the future. The "level of affiliation" may approximately be judged by analyzing the pattern of the signing of major documents.

Results are shown in *table 3* (minor irregularities in signing patterns must be admitted, though they primarily occurred with less important documents).

De jure affiliation is not, of course, an absolute or constant indicator of a republic's level of allegiance to the CIS. It may be higher or lower within the same legal framework depending on to what extent the assumed obligations are being honored (failure to deliver promised goods may not always be a deliberate policy).

At present the core of political and military integration within the Commonwealth is formed by the signatories to the Agreement on Collective Security in May 1992. Top CIS military officials are not inclined to see this accord as establishing a formal security pact[1]. They are right in the sense that it will take time and much effort to make the agreement work: to further harmonize foreign and security policies by the participants, to actually act on the treaty translating its "structural" clauses into reality (i.e., to set up the Collective Security Coun-

---

[1] General Samsonov, CIS Joint Armed Forces Chief of Staff, remarked, that the treaty only "forms the basis for a defensive alliance". – Krasnaya Zvevda, July 3, 1992.

cil, to get it working, to establish extra links between the CIS High Command and the treaty member states etc.), and above all to make the participants aware of the accord as a binding document, not merely a declaration of intent[2].

The future may bring changes in the republics' politico-military "allegiances" (de facto and/or de jure) to the CIS structures and institutions due to a wide variety of reasons, analyzed below.

In recent months **Belarus** has moved much closer to the CIS and especially to Russia. Talks in July 1992 between Stanislav Shushkevitch and Yegor Gaidar on economic, political and military, including nuclear, issues sparked off rumors about a Russian and Belarus confederation. And it was widely expected that sooner rather than later Belarus would join the Collective Security Agreement. However, Minsk was clearly disappointed by the Russian-Ukrainian settlement of the Black Sea fleet issue outside the CIS framework (which was regarded as a precedent for going back on one's pledges, and as a move depriving Belarus of its fair share of the fleet). This unhappy development combined with strong pressure from the opposition will force Stanislav Shushkevitch to "freeze" a further integration of the republic in the CIS and forging closer links to Russia.

Pressed by economic, military and political realities, President Leonid Kravtchuk of **Ukraine** is drifting closer to Russia and the CIS, but in this movement he is hamstrung by a still powerful opposition and his personal ambitions. Therefore in the near future Ukraine is unlikely to get much deeper involved in the CIS security structures than it is today. The reverse movement looks more feasible. Here much will depend on the performance of the opposition. It is now less united (and more diversified in its approach towards the CIS) compared to the situation at the beginning of 1992, but it may still present multiple surprises. The victory of the opposition or even its greater influence over the president may reverse, possibly to the breaking point, those rather few but still important agreements that bind Ukraine to the CIS (nuclear matters are of particular importance here).

Tajikistan's position at the heart of the CIS security alliance is jeopardized by an internal political strife and the removal of President Nabiyev who is widely seen as the main driving force behind the republic's entry into the CIS and its place there. With the opposition having won the upper hand in the capital and the civil war raging, Tajikistan will still most likely stay formally on where it is in integration

---

[2] So far this awareness is mostly lacking, the point being exemplified by the failure to invoke the Agreement at the request of Armenia in August, when the Azeri forces reportedly invaded the Armenian territory.

terms. But its security contribution to the CIS is sure to be frozen. A de-jure reduction in the affiliation level up to complete withdrawal may occur only in the unlikely case of the country's getting under total Islamic control and forging close ties to Islamic states across the border. In any contingency, Tajikistan's close proximity to China and overhanging threat of being divided between more powerful neighbors will act as a strong "integrating factor".

A calm but tense situation prevails in **Uzbekistan** threatening to split the republic (which is a rather artificial entity), with nationalist and Islamic forces waiting on the sidelines to step in and move the republic (in the whole or in parts) closer to the Islamic south away from the CIS.

As of today, **Moldavian** participation in the CIS is largely nominal. The Moldavian President is under heavy pressure to cut the tenuous links to the CIS in favor of joining the "Greater Rumania". Though two prominent "hawks" have been ousted from the government in July, the militancy may well surge up in the leadership again (when, for instance, Kishinev eventually gets peace in its troubled provinces), and the republic may try to withdraw from the CIS. This move will inevitably lead to the renewed armed confrontation between Kishinev and Tiraspol (the Gagauz Republic may also be involved), and Russia will be hard-pressed to intervene militarily.

Armenia may eventually get disenchanted with Russia's failure to lend it a helping hand in its struggle with Azerbaijan under the terms of the Collective Security Agreement. Great disappointment may lead Armenia to de-facto reduce its "security profile" in the CIS (Given its largely hostile "surroundings," it is unlikely to break out of the collective security structure altogether, at least until the war with Azerbaijan rages on).

For ideological reasons, **Azerbaijan** would rather opt to stay out of the CIS structures. But for the time being it will most likely stay on waiting until the prospects for its conflict with Armenia get clearer, and its relations with Turkey mature, in order to lessen the economic dependence on Russia and the CIS. Azerbaijan may declare its renewed interest in the CIS and even the Collective Security Agreement to force Armenia to quit them.

Initially **Turkmenistan** showed a surprising proclivity to autonomy within the CIS (probably motivated by huge oil and gas resources). But of late President Sapurmurad Niyazov has moved closer to Russia, signing a number of vital bilateral agreements. It may well happen that this new proximity will show itself in Turkmenistan's closer security integration with the CIS and its joining the Collective Security Agreement at a later stage.

The CIS security framework has already been strengthened by a series of bilateral security/military and friendship/cooperation agreements (between Russia and Armenia, Russia and Belarus, Russia and Turkmenistan). This trend will not only continue but intensify, because it is much easier to reconcile two sets of interests than many ones. Somewhere in the future bilateral agreements could involve non-members of the CIS, especially those whose territory accommodates joint CIS strategic and/or Russian military bases and installations.[3]

The third issue for analysis is the prospective military organization of the CIS and problems associated with it. The proposed CIS defense structure is depicted in *Chart 1*.

In general, it may be a workable and lasting arrangement. But still its "operational efficiency" can not be taken for granted. Major sticking points and bottlenecks, analyzed below, should be taken seriously for the CIS to be a success in security terms.

There are at least three issues of principle that deserve close scrutiny:

a. In order to survive, any alliance or association should enjoy unanimity or close proximity of views and attitudes, which is not the case with the CIS now. Differing political wills, which dominate the Commonwealth, may well get in the way of taking security decisions or hamper their implementation. An easy victim to clashing political attitudes, for instance, may be the "internal" peace-keeping force, which in most cases will act against at least one side's preferences and expectations. (That is why it may be strongly recommended that their actual application should be decided on a "consensus minus one" basis.) So, harmonization of foreign and security policies by the CIS members is a vital condition to get the CIS military organization fully "off the ground", but one cannot expect this to happen in the near and even medium term.

b. Any military machinery cannot properly function without a legal "charter". As the CIS is not a formal political and military alliance, it cannot have a full-fledged military doctrine. It will have to confine itself to a comprehensive set of principles of action, specifying the member states' behavior (individual and collective) in the security area. These principles are not yet worked out, and they will be difficult to achieve given wide disagreements in the CIS on future ways of the Commonwealth. (In the opinion of Marshal Shaposh-

---

[3] For instance, at the press-conference in the wake of the Moscow summit Marshal Shaposhnikov spoke of the need to conclude an agreement with Latvia covering a space/air defence related installation on its territory. (ITAR-TASS Script, July 8, 1992, p. 2.) Surely, similar installations in other Baltic republics and in Georgia will have to be similarly covered.

nikov, the CIS C-in-C, the Collective Security arrangement may in the future be transformed into a CIS-based political-military or military-political alliance with a coalition doctrine[4]. This is probably, a too optimistic and far-off scenario: its implementation must be preceded by harmonizing the foreign policy and security goals of the member states, which cannot be done right away, or at all.)

c. It is now clear that the CIS military organization will have to live side by side with national armies, which are practically being created by all member states. These armies will greatly differ in nature and composition, ranging from 1.5 million people in Russia to small para-military formations and national guards in Central Asia. It is hard to believe that "cohabitation" of the CIS and national structures can proceed peacefully on its own. Thus, it will be necessary to differentiate areas of responsibility between them and to work out guidelines for future cooperation. It seems to be a formidable job, since only Russia and to some extent Belarus, Kazakhstan and the Central Asian republics are on speaking terms with the CIS military establishment. (Note that the issue of nuclear weapons control within the CIS has not been settled, despite clear lines drawn in *Chart 1*, and a number of agreements reached on the nuclear issue.[5] Ukraine is still the biggest question mark. With its eventual political will as to the nuclear or non-nuclear status apparently undecided, the CIS C-in-C has already been left with only operational control of the Strategic Nuclear Forces on the Ukrainian territory after being deprived of administrative command authority.)

The other side of this problem is how to deal with multiple illegal para-military groups that infest the territory of certain CIS member states. Probably no government within the CIS harbors good feelings towards them, but no government has political will and/or military capability to cope with them. It can be easily predicted that such illegal armed groupings will grow in number, motivated, on the one hand, by mounting political, economic, ethnic, and other problems, and on the other hand by the easy access to weapons stocks. It seems that in several years the CIS leaders will have to sit down and discuss what they can collectively do with these destabilizing "irritants".

The discussed scheme of future military cooperation within the CIS also has some "structural" deficiencies, which may hamper its smooth performance:

---

[4] Izvestiya, July 3, 1992.
[5] For more information and analysis of the issue see: K. Sorokin. Soviet Strategic Legacy. – Mirovaya Economica i Mezhdunarodniye Otnosheniya (World economy and international relations), N 4, 1992, pp. 51–65.

- The proposed CIS "Nuclear Planning Group" is to include the signatories of the Collective Security Agreement and the states that house nuclear weapons. Such composition of the group keeps out with immediate effect Azerbaijan, Moldova and Turkmenistan (and probably Ukraine and Belarus if and when they obtain a non-nuclear status), threatening more painful fissions in the CIS. (The Belarus and Turkmenian "case" may be settled if they both join the Collective-Security-Framework, but such a solution will not seem suitable to the other three.)
- Russian Air Defence, Air Force and Naval Commanders will simultaneously hold the positions as C-in-Cs AD, AF and Naval Deputies. This arrangement is unlikely to go well with the republics, which have decided to place their military units under joint operational command, causing at least a latent discontent and probably a risk of such units' withdrawal. It also sours the prospects for the Ukrainian, Azeri, and Moldavian national military contingents to ever be drawn in the joint operational command network.
- Conspicuous by their absence in *chart 1* are (a) the CIS General Purpose Forces Commander and (b) the C-in-C Land Forces Deputy. The latter case is probably best explained by most republics' desire to keep their land troops (which are least dependent on outside material and technical assistance) to themselves as the most reliable guarantors of their unique national interests. Instead, the CIS members have reached a preliminary agreement on a shadowy collective force for a local conflicts resolution along external borders, which was the most they could settle on in the land forces domain.[6] And the absence of a GPF Commander post is an added indicator that joint GPF are not and probably never will be a full-blooded reality, at least for some time to come.
- It is still far from clear what will be the size of the Joint Forces. The now freewheeling republics started setting their own military targets, bound only by international accords (Kazakhstan and the Central Asian republics are not members of the CFE process) and poor economic capabilities. However, in order to improve the intra-CIS coordination and to prevent possible military build-up excesses, as well as to avoid scaring close neighbors in and outside of the Commonwealth, it would be wise to try to put some binding figures on the future size of the joint forces.
- The Russian-Ukrainian settlement of the Black Sea fleet issue outside the CIS framework has helped to defuse tension between the

---

[6] It is not yet clear whether paratroopers and border guards will be included under a joint umbrella.

two, but created an unfortunate precedent for breaking earlier pledges and keeping Strategic Forces formations outside the joint security structure.

Ambiguities and future hardships notwithstanding, it is impossible to turn the clock back and rejuvenate the Soviet army-type single armed forces. Under the optimistic scenario one can calculate at closer integration of several national armed forces within the Collective Security framework, as well as gradual increase in the membership of this agreement which will become the real core of the CIS. The pessimistic scenario (which is highly unlikely) will include the demise of the CIS in its present form, which may not affect some elements of its military security structure (i.e. the Agreement on Collective Security, signed by the six republics in May 1992 in Tashkent, or bilateral friendship and security treaties between the CIS members). The most likely scenario will be the retention of the CIS security structure in its present semi-defined and semi-operating mode for the years to come with occasional improvements and deteriorations in its performance.

The Russian Army: Created and Reformed

The Russian army is not only the protector from outside aggression and interference, but a vital instrument to prevent it from following the path of the Soviet Union. In the gloomy atmosphere of overall internal crisis and mounting economic and political separatism in the provinces, the army will sometimes be the only reliable political and moral link between various parts of the country. In this sense the creation of the national armed forces was a welcome development, because the unimpeded disintegration of Russia will probably lead to a civil war with potentially grave consequences. Russian armed forces are being created under the Presidential Directive of May 7, 1992. At present they include all armed formations and military institutions of the former Soviet Army on Russian territory (all strategic nuclear offensive and strategic defensive forces;[7] general purpose forces, grouped in seven military districts; Northern and Far Eastern fleets[8]) plus groups of forces, armed formations, bases, military installations and other defence institutions of the Red Army located outside the Russian territory, not claimed by other former Soviet republics and

---

[7] The Russian leadership believes, that by the year 2000 strategic and tactical nuclear forces in Russia will be the only such forces in the CIS. (See B. Yeltsin's interview in Komsomolskaya Pravda, May 27 1992; Gen. P. Grachev's interview in Krasnaya Zvezda, June 6, 1992.)

[8] It is estimated that some 90–92 percent of the former Soviet Navy are based on Russian soil. (Krasnaya Zvezda, May 21, 1992.)

taken under the Russian control (the Western Group of forces in Germany due to be withdrawn to Russia by the end of 1994; the Northern Group of forces in Poland to be fully withdrawn at approximately the same time; the North-Western Group of forces in the Baltic region and the Kaliningrad area plus the Baltic fleet[9]; the Transcaucasian military district[10]; the 14th Army in Moldova due to be withdrawn by a yet unspecified date; a naval base on the Caspian Sea left over to Russia following the division of the Caspian flotilla; some forces in Central Asia[11]; and some military bases outside the borders of the former Soviet Union[12]). All the Russian forces classed as "strategic" under the CIS Agreement on the Strategic Forces, signed in Minsk on December 30, 1991, will be kept under operational control of the CIS High Command.[13] The Black Sea fleet will be jointly possessed and controlled by Russia and Ukraine outside the CIS structure until its division between the two in 1995.

Though the sheer size of the force under Russian control is considerable, their readiness and combat effectiveness should be generally described as low. Firstly, it is mostly composed of odd parts of what once was a single army, which often do not form homogeneous military structures. Secondly, Russian-controlled forces are beset by formidable shortcomings in financial, logistical supply, low morale, by demographic, psychological and other problems. Relatively effective today are strategic nuclear, anti-ballistic missile and air-defence systems. The general purpose forces still are in a much poorer shape.[14]

In Russia's future is to have a smaller, cheaper but more modern and capable army. So far there is a set of general ideas on how to restructure the existing armed forces and what they should look like by the target date, the year 2000. However, there is no single plan on this score (which will probably have to be ratified by the parliament), and

---

[9] Moscow proposes to withdraw its troops from the three Baltic republics by 1995, but the Baltic governments insist on a much earlier date (the future of Russian forces in the Kaliningrad area is still undecided).

[10] It is believed, that the Russian forces in Azerbaijan will be the first to withdraw, while in Armenia and Georgia Russian troops may stay longer on request of the two republics' governments, if they manage to stop the surge of violence directed against these troops. In any case, the greatest part of their weapons and military equipment will be left to the three republics.

[11] The Uzbec government has asked the Russian troops to stay indefinitely on. (B. Yeltsin's interview in Komsomolskaya Pravda, July 3, 1992).

[12] I.e., the base in Cam Ran, Vietnam. (See: Izvestiya, July 23, 1992.)

[13] SRNF, Air Force, Navy, Air Defence, space forces, air-borne troops and related institutions; nuclear warheads guardians; strategic and operational-level intelligence. – Diplomatichesky Vestnik (Diplomatic herald), N 2–3, 1992, p. 10.

[14] As A. Rutzkoi, the Vice-President, put it, the existing "armed formations can hardly be called the Army. Command and control systems as well as weapons do not live up to modern standards". (Voyennaya Mysl (The Military Thought), Special edition, July 1992, p. 44.)

views expressed in different military quarters sometimes do not square with each other. Still one can already ascertain basic principles, which will underlie the prospective military reform:
- Drastic reductions in the size of the active armed forces. By May 1, 1992 the strength of the Russian-controlled forces totalled 2800 thousand servicemen, 2200 thousand of which were located on the Russian territory. By 1995 the Army is to be reduced to 2.1 million troops, and to 1.5 million by the year 2000.[15]
- Gradual evolution in the present mixed system of manning the army (conscripts and professional officers). It is assumed that the share of professionals will grow, but it is not yet clear whether conscription will eventually survive.
- Eventual withdrawal of the bulk of Russian forces from abroad, and adoption of "defence from within the national borders".
- Abandonment of the concept of a strong echeloned and continuous layer of defence along the borders, which is impossible to implement, given the length of the frontiers, the lack of adequate material and financial resources and the dwindling size of the army. Instead, Russia is to rely on mobile defense with effective mobile forces capable of being quickly moved to the endangered areas at its heart.[16]
- A smaller but more effective and flexible system of command and control is to be established.[17]
- Speedy development of "the high-tech Services", i.e. the Air Force, the Navy, the SRNF, Space Systems Commands and the Air Defense,[18] while the tank-heavy Land Forces (tailored to fight a major war in Europe) will be substantially reduced and reorganized with top priority given to mobile units best suited for most probable local conflicts. Mobile forces ("strategic-operational level large units") will be made of air-borne troops, marine infantry and light army formations, helicopter and army aviation squadrons, military transport planes, etc.[19]
- General administrative division of the army into Strategic Deterrence Forces (SDF) and General Purpose Forces (GPF).

[15] Statement by the General Staff representative General V. Barinkin to the Parliament on May 12, 1992.
[16] A. Kokoshin (deputy Defense Minister) in: Izvestiya, July 20, 1992. The Vice-President A. Rutzkoi stands for an "impregnable shield" along the borders (Krasnaya Zvezda, May 22, 1992), but it looks more like a metaphor.
[17] The size of the Russian MOD and General Staff may not exceed 4-7 thousand people, which is a 3-4 times drop compared to the corresponding Soviet structures. (Krasnaya Zvezda, March 31, 1992). By the year 2000 the Services Commands may be transformed into much smaller departments within the MOD. (Krasnaya Zvezda, July 21, 1992.)
[18] A. Kokoshin in: Krasnaya Zvezda, March 17 and June 23, 1992.
[19] Krasnaya Zvezda, July 21, 1992.

- Within Operational Commands, the GPF will be grouped according to their mission into covering constant readiness forces (along borders), tasked to deter/repel local aggression on a limited scale; mobile (rapid reaction) forces, located further inland and capable to be speedily moved to a threatened area to augment the covering forces, in order to beat off a medium-sized aggression, and if necessary to enable a safe deployment of reserves; and reserve forces, mobilized and deployed in a short war period or during the war to stand up to a larger attack.[20]
- Overall switch to producing lesser amounts of weapons, with advanced technology weapons to be accorded top priority.

The above principles are to be put to life in three stages, with the third and final one due to end around the year 2000. The projected shape of the Russian Army by the turn of the century is shown in *chart 2*.

In creating the new army, the present Russian leadership will have to get to grips with the huge deficit of financial and material resources. It is impossible that the crisis-struck nation can muster all the resources required to carry out the reform. Defense expenditures have already been declining in real terms for some years[21] and are likely to go down still further.

The lack of financial resources may have another even worse consequence. The decision to create the national army raised hopes among the officers for a quick improvement in their social and housing conditions. If their hopes are dashed, and things seem to be quickly moving in this direction, then the army may easily get out of control with unpredictable consequences: probably, there won't be a force to cope with the well-organized and armed groups of disillusioned officers.

Yet another is the personnel problem. At present the army suffers from low morale, depletion of the officer corps, internal ethnic tensions, and growing shortage and declining quality of conscripts. The first, second and to some extent third "ailments" can be cured provided there is an upturn in the economy. But the fourth one is of profound and long standing nature.

The most likely scenario is that by the year 2000 Russia will go some way but not all the way towards implementing military reform. How far the reform will go, depends on the socio-economic, political and demographic situation in the country (provided the situation abroad remains largely unchanged). The only alternative, barring the complete disintegration of Russia and collapse of its armed forces, is

---

[20] Voyennaya Mysl, Special edition, July 1992, pp. 56–57.
[21] By 2.5 times in 1992 compared to 1990. – Voyennaya Mysl, Special edition, July 1992, p. 47.

the return to the traditional Soviet ways: should the present democratic leadership be removed by neo-communist and ultra-nationalist forces, the whole idea of military reform will most surely go away together with its backers. But probably in any case the future Russian army will still be a force to be reckoned with, sustained by at least a residual nuclear arsenal.

5. The Political Situation in Russia

The breakup of communism in Russia resulted in the disintegration of the "democratic" coalition opposing the Communist Party, an ad hoc political instrument. This was a rule in all anti-totalitarian revolutions. But while in the countries of East and Central Europe these developments laid the basis for building a multiparty system, the "democratic split" in Russia virtually outstripped the rise of a multiparty system and of the new power structure. Indeed, the ideas of a democracy and parliamentarianism have been partly discredited even before they were put into practice.

Political Party Forces

The established post-communist regime is a fragile, unstable and insufficiently legitimate power structure that is made up of essentially different elements. The president, the government, and heads of local authorities have no party affiliation. The supreme body of power was also elected on a non-party basis in 1990, though the state system and social order have radically changed since then.

The supreme body of power has a peculiar configuration. It is composed of the Congress of People's Deputies (there are 1049 of them)[22] that elects the Supreme Soviet (248 deputies: 124 in the Soviet of the Republic, and 124 in the Soviet of Nationalities). Vast powers are invested in this jumbo congress, periodically called for sessions. The authority of the standing and relatively small Supreme Soviet is restricted. The factions of the Parliament (of both the Congress and the Supreme Soviet) have only indirect connection (i.e. social and ideological empathy) with the existent political parties, and only several dozens of deputies have a party affiliation. The activity of the main

---

[22] In April 1992 19 seats of 1068 were vacant.

parties themselves (there are about 20, with the total number reaching several hundreds) has little impact on the deputies or factions. For example, the six deputies of the Democratic Party of Russia enter into four different factions.

As for the parties, one can outline five principal political tendencies:

1. **Organizations of a communist and left-wing socialist trend**, based on the orthodox cadre of the former CPSU that were created after the ban of the Communist Party in late 1991 – early 1992 (The All-Union Communist Party (Bolshevik) of N. Andreyeva (VKPb); The Russian Communist Workers Party of A. Makashov and V. Anpilov; The Workers' and Peasants' Socialist Party of S. Gubanov; The Union of Communists of A. Prigarin; The Russian Party of Communists of A. Kryuchkov; The Party of Labor of B. Kagarlitsky and A. Buzgalin; the Socialist Workers' Party of A. Denisov and R. Medvedev). According to public opinion polls, communist parties are supported only by several percent of the population. However, they have inherited from the CPSU a disproportionate share of representatives in both the federal parliament (in the "Communists of Russia" faction and others like "Fatherland", "Russia" and "The Agrarian Union", teaming up with it), and the local legislatures and administrations.
2. **Parties of a left-centrist kind**, from Social Democrats to left-Liberals, supported by the reformist wing of the former Communist Party, by pragmatically-minded intelligentsia, and by the directors' and engineers' corps (The People's Party of Free Russia of A. Rutskoi and V. Lipitsky; The Democratic Party of Russia of N. Travkin; the All-Russian Union "Renewal" of A. Volsky and A. Vladislavlev that emerged from the Union of Industrialists and Entrepreneurs, uniting the directors of major state enterprises). These three groups formed the "Civic Union". Each of these parties has a local network and a solid base in such parliamentary factions as "Free Russia", *"Smena"*, "The Industrial Union", "The Worker's Union", "Sovereignty and Equality", and the "Nonparty Members".
3. Ideologically akin to the second tendency but politically separated from it is **a group of small parties that were formerly a part of the "Democratic Russia" movement** (The Republican Party of the Russian Federation of V. Lysenko and V. Shostakovsky; The Social-Democratic Party of Russia of O. Rumyantsev and B. Orlov; The Peasants' Party of Yu. Chernitchenko; The People's Party of T. Gdlyan). These small parties are to some extent represented in the parliament by the "Left Center" faction.

4. **The liberal-democratic tendency**, which is closer to conservatives in the traditional sense, supported by Western-oriented intelligentsia and part of the business circles. Their organizational basis is the decaying "Democratic Russia" movement that still retains a relatively strong position in the parliament (factions "Radical Democrats" and "Democratic Russia", with the partial support of "Sovereignty and Equality" and non-party factions). A new phenomenon on the political scene is the "Party of Economic Liberty" headed by K. Borovoy, S. Fedorov and I. Hakamada. This party is the organization of the new bourgeoisie. By the end of 1992 several political groups of entrepreneurs and liberal parliamentarians, the Republican Party, which is rapidly moving to the right, the Party of Economic Liberty some people around the former Prime Minister E. Gaidar and moderate factions of the "Democratic Russia" movement started with the creation of a liberal center-right coalition to balance and to compete with the "Civic Union".
5. **The extreme right of the political spectrum**, politically close to the extreme left, is occupied by organizations and movements that define themselves as national-patriotic (The Union of People's Patriotic Forces of Russia of G. Ziuganov; The Russian Nation-wide Union of S. Baburin and S. Pavlov; The Russian National *Sobor* (Council) of A. Sterligov and V. Rasputin; The Russian People's Assembly of I. Konstantinov; The Constitutional Democratic Party of M. Astafyev; and the Russian Christian Democratic Movement of V. Aksiuchits). The social base of these movements is nationalistic-minded part of intelligentsia and of the former Communist Party apparatus, as well as marginal elements of the population. In the parliament they are backed by the factions "Fatherland" and "Communists of Russia", and partially supported by the factions "Russia" and "The Agrarian Union".

The date of birth of each political party was the time of withdrawal of its founders from the Communist Party. The first wave of apostates made up the leadership of "Democratic Russia", the second wave (called "The Democratic Platform within the CPSU") transformed into the Republican Party, and the third wave ("Communists for Democracy") laid the basis for the "People's Party of Free Russia".

The majority of political parties have been formed not on the basis of common interest, but rather on a vague proximity of opinions and as a rule have consolidated around certain political figures. The distinctions between parties are mostly insignificant, and their fractional existence can only be explained by their leaders' ambitions, hence frequent splits within the parties and the permanent change of allies.

The activity of most parties is limited to Moscow, St. Peterbourg, and several major cities, and it is increasingly restricted by the new trend of regional autonomy. As a matter of fact, all existent parties are crippled due to their small size, scarce financing, the lack of state support, limited intellectual potential, the absence of prominent leaders, and the weakness of party structures. They did not take their time to become sound political forces and actually remained protoparties.

While prior to August 1991 the "democratic" forces were on the rise, constantly winning new allies to their cause, the situation radically changed in fall and winter of 1991-1992. The "democratic" wing suffered multiple splits and withdrawals and practically lost its ability to rally people. The denial of "democratic" affiliation became a political *bon ton*, and parties and politicians that were earlier considered "democratic" were hastily making statements of a "patriotic" character. In the meanwhile, the national-patriotic and communist forces started to consolidate their ranks, increased their political activities, and proved able to launch relatively massive drives of protest.

In June 1992 the "Democratic Party of Russia" of N. Travkin, the People's Party of Free Russia of A. Rutskoi, and the All-Russian Union 'Renewal' of A. Volsky joined to form the "Civic Union". Thus the centrist opposition to the Gaidar cabinet has been finally molded. The Social-Democratic Party and Republican Party, too, began to keep away from the government, and even "Democratic Russia" started to criticize certain aspects of the governmental policies.

At present there are three major political forces in the parliament:
- the opposition bloc that is highly critical of the president, the government and the current regime in general (the factions "Communists of Russia", "Fatherland", "The Agrarian Union" and "Russia");
- a group of factions that conditionally support the president and are mostly critical of the government ("The Industrial Union", "The Workers' Union", *"Smena"* and "Sovereignty and Equality");
- six factions that are loyal to the president and the government, of which four are members of the bloc of democratic factions.

It is quite evident that the political evolution and the regrouping of parties will dramatically reduce the parliamentary base of the government. The centrist "Civic Union" has formed its bloc of factions called "The Democratic Center". As a matter of fact, "The Civic Union" has taken a key position in the parliament and has the decisive say in the argument between the reformers and the opposition. Such advantageous a situation will win them new supporters from both the right and the left. "The Civic Union" has been taking a stand of a "constructive opposition" to the cabinet and demanding to "adjust" the current reformist course in the latest period.

The semi-phyrric victory of the "Civic Union" at the December 1992 Congress of the People's Deputies with the installment of the Prime Minister, connected with the "Civic Union", but with the retention of the key figures of the Gaidar cabinet, is bound to produce cracks in the ranks of the "Union". The "whitening" (moving into the class of bourgeoisie) of many of the former "red directors" will facilitate this split.

Internal Tensions in Russia's Government

The situation in high echelons of power is also rather intricate. Though Alexander Rutskoi became vice-president on the same ballot with Boris Yeltsin and proved to be a devoted supporter of the president in the days of the August coup, their ways began to part since fall 1991. The speaker of the parliament Ruslan Khasbulatov, another close ally, who actually owes his office to the president and to democratic forces, also began to take a separate political stand at about this time. While remaining seemingly loyal to B.Yeltsin, both A. Rutskoi and R. Khasbulatov criticize the government headed by the president.

In the meanwhile, the Central Bank, controlled by the parliament, attempts to frustrate the fiscal policies of the government aimed at stabilizing the national currency. Heads of local administrations, appointed personally by Boris Yeltsin, also have little confidence in the government. According to the poll held in May 1992, 17 percent of them deemed the government incompetent, 60 percent supposed that it had lost control over the events, and 70 to 80 percent were dissatisfied by its fiscal, credit, and tax policies.[23]

The evolution of the executive branch itself is quite remarkable. The president attempted to merge the Ministries of Security and of the Interior by a special directive in December 1991, but the Constitutional Court outlawed this action. The border troops, though, that were supposed to become an independent service, were turned over to the Ministry of Security. In April 1992 the Security Council, hitherto nominal, appeared on the political scene. The secretary of this body with vast and obscure powers was appointed Yuri Skokov, a figure admitted to military-industrial circles, and supposedly a personal

---

[23] Megapolis-Express, 1992, May 27.

friend of the Minister of Defense. Gennadi Burbulis and Sergei Shakhrai, influential representatives of democratic forces in B.Yeltsin's team, resigned from the posts of vice-premiers and from the government, and advisers to the president from the academic milieu acquired a lower profile. At the same time people from the president's staff and from 'the Sverdlovsk apparatchiks' moved to the positions of influence.

After appointments of general Pavel Grachev as the Minister of Defense, of general Boris Gromov as his deputy, and a major reshuffle in the Ministry of Defense, the key positions in the armed forces were occupied by the "Afghan lobby", presumed to be somewhat sympathetic of the national-patriotic forces. Further on, in May and June 1992 the reorganization of the Cabinet was taking place, during which the key posts of vice-premiers were given to practicing managers from the directors' corps. And finally, the latest amendments of B.Yeltsin to the draft of the Constitution (the draft was already providing for the presidential-parliamentary form of government) envisage the presidential rule for the entire "transitional period" without any serious checks.[24]

Boris Yeltsin is thus undoubtedly inclined to a strong presidential rule of an authoritarian kind. Recent changes in the executive branch – the advancement of the Ministries of Defense and Security and of the state apparatus, the replacement of "democratic" figures by nomenclatura cadre, complete disregard of opinions of both the opposition and the "democrats" – clearly testify to this authoritarian drift.

The events in the parliament that is supposed to counterbalance the authoritarian ambitions of the president, take a very similar turn. A number of moves made by the speaker Ruslan Khasbulatov during 1992 were aimed at turning the Supreme Soviet into a kind of powerful ministry headed by the speaker, with the activity of the deputies controlled by the loyal apparatus. Added to this are relentless attempts of R. Khasbulatov to bring one of the most popular Russian newspapers, well respected all over the former USSR, *"Izvestiya"*, under his personal control.

Drawing a parallel, the policies of Boris Yeltsin actually resemble those of Mikhail Gorbachev in spring 1991, and Ruslan Khasbulatov quite realistically plays the role of Anatoly Lukyanov. The new coup will probably not be needed, because opposing forces, coming from different sides and seeking their specific goals, are jointly creating the mechanism of authoritarian power. The December 1992 Congress, where by ill-conceived tactics and mistakes the president has

---

[24] Nezavisimaya Gazeta, 1992, August 26.

undermined his position and standing and weakened the power of the executive, has most probably strengthened this tendency in the medium (though not in the short) term.

Phase of New Orientation in Nomenclatura and the Academic Intelligentsia

Characteristic changes are taking place in the social base of the regime. The nomenclatura has recovered from the August shock and has accommodated in the new political environment. Getting rid of ideolog-minded apparatchiks that could not reconcile themselves to the new regime and therefore joined the 'red-and-brown' opposition, the state and industrial nomenclatura has consolidated its ranks. It has occupied approaches to power and is ready for political comeback.

In the meanwhile, by summer 1992, the regime actually lost the support of the academic and artistic intelligentsia, that championed the anti-nomenklatura drive. The grievous situation in science and culture that became first victims of market reforms, a drastic decline of the social profile of the intelligentsia, and its utter impoverishment, as well as the disappointment in the new authorities that turned out to be professionally and morally unsound, has pushed the main supporting social force away from the regime.

Public sentiments have also considerably changed over the last year. With price liberalization, the overwhelming majority of the population can hardly make ends meet. As clearly shown by the polls, any new rise in prices results in the growth of social discontent. By September 1992, 36 percent of Moscow residents could not sustain the price liberalization (46 percent in late January, 33 percent in late February, 42 percent in late March, 40 percent in early April, 37 percent in June, 32 percent in August). 65 percent of Muscovites were dissatisfied with their life in September 1992 (81 percent in late January, 68 percent in late February, 74 percent in late March, 73 percent in early April, 73 percent in June, 63 percent in August).[25] In this sense the economic policies of the government are dangerously close to the "red line", beyond which the social costs of the reform will prove unacceptable for the overwhelming majority of the population.

The basic political capital of the government, and of reformist forces in general, has been the popular confidence in Boris Yeltsin. In the meanwhile, according to the polls, the rating of the president has

[25] Izvestiya, 1992, February 10, 24, April 6, June 29, September 7.

considerably declined. 54 percent of Muscovites trusted Boris Yeltsin in February 1992, 57 percent in April, 32 percent in May, and 23 percent in June.[26] 46 percent of Muscovites did not believe in the success of his economic policies in January 1992, 49 percent in March, 50 percent in May to August, and 58 percent in September. The number of supporters of these policies went down from 38 percent in January 1992 to 26 percent in September.[27] After the above-mentioned defeat at the December 1992 Congress the President suffered an additional loss of confidence.

The disillusionment in state authorities and "democratic forces" is quite apparent. In February 1992 25 percent of Muscovites pinned their hopes to get out of the crisis on the current administration, and 9 percent on "democratic forces", 14 percent and 10 percent accordingly in June, and 19 percent and 11 percent in August.[28] Public confidence in the parliament and in political parties is even lower.[29] The number of Muscovites satisfied with the work of the parliament went down from 16 percent (and 62 percent dissatisfied) in March 1992 to 5 percent (and 56 percent dissatisfied) in September.[30] This actually means that not only the cabinet and the president, but the entire political system has lost its constituency. Such a situation is certainly favorable for the strengthening of authoritarian tendencies. However, no forces are in sight which could introduce a strong, rather than a weak authoritarian regime.

The Acceptance of the New Political System by the Citizens

The polls show, however, that the loss of public confidence for the "democratic forces" does not mean any significant increase in popularity of their opponents, the communist and national-patriotic forces. The growth of social tensions is accompanied not by the increase of political tension but rather by political passivity of the population. Given this, the opposition can hardly expect to receive popular support.

Political passivity of the masses against the background of extreme social tension often foreshadows a social upheaval. Massive social and economic protests can grow into a politically indifferent or a politically biased riot. The main factors of social destabilization are:

---

[26] Izvestiya, 1992, May 30, June 29.
[27] Izvestiya, 1992, September 7.
[28] Izvestiya, 1992, June 29, August 24.
[29] Nezavisimaya Gazeta, 1992, May 30, August 22.
[30] Izvestiya, 1992, September 14.

(a) massive unemployment; (b) a new drastic fall of the living standards; (c) an immense inflow of refugees from the former USSR republics;[31] (d) the failure and discrediting of the privatization program. On the other hand, in the situation of total political indifference, the population might not even notice the degeneration of power and the institutional coup at the top.

The main point is that making a break in reforms, and temporarily relieving social tension, any new more conservative government will soon be facing exactly the same problems, further complicated by hyperinflation. This brings about the question of a "third cabinet", or rather cabinets, which will be able to start introducing lasting changes. However, the political life is so intensive that by the time this question becomes practical, the actors and setting on the political scene will change almost completely. One can only outline the principal factors of political differentiation.

One of the main factors will be the chosen model and the actual manner of privatization. They will define the nature of property and of the social structure, as well as the very type of the emerging new society – African, Latin American or European – will be competing the supporters of "popular", "nomenklatura", and "private-property" privatization.

Another point of political confrontation is the question of the nature of political power in Russia – democratic or authoritarian, parliamentary or presidential. The present divisions on this issue are temporary. It is worth noticing, that "democrats" are now most ardent supporters of an authoritarian rule and the readers of *"Pravda"* are champions of democracy.

The third factor of political differentiation is the debate on the future state arrangement in Russia (federalist, confederalist, or unitarian), its role in the CIS, and the nature of the Commonwealth. The discussion will be further fueled by ethnic conflicts on the territory of the former USSR and in Russia itself and by the ever increasing flow of Russian and Russian-speaking refugees and migrants. The general political drift towards the "imperial" side is quite foreseeable. There may be certain unexpected turns, though. Some "democrats" are already going national-patriotic. Also feasible is the emergence of Russian nationalism not of an expansionist but of an isolationist kind (under the influence of, say, the ideas of Alexander Solzhenitzyn). Another sphere of political differentiation is the foreign policy of Russia.

---

[31] At present there are 300 thousand registered refugees in Russia, and the number of unregistered refugees is estimated from 1 to 2,8 million (Izvestiya, 1992, September 18).

It is quite apparent that the existent political spectrum can not adequately express the future differentiation of interests, ideologies, and political forces. This can lead to a radical reshuffle of all current political tendencies, parties, and coalitions, in which there will be hardly any continuity or even to such a radical rearrangement on the political scene that is better described by the final stage direction in Shakespeare's *"Hamlet":* "Exeunt, bearing off the dead bodies".

6. The Political Situation in the CIS Countries

The Russocentric Character of the CIS

The political situation in the republics of the former Soviet Union is largely explained by a paradox: *what broke up in December 1991 was the state, but not the country.* Having obtained independence, the majority of republics remained quasi-state entities (much like South African Bantustans), yet incapable of effective exercise of elementary state functions.

The internal processes in the newly formed states have much in the common. The post-Soviet era has retained a high degree of economic, political, and military dependence on Russia, while ambitious attempts to break this dependence make it even more apparent. Relentless efforts of the Baltic states to shut themselves off from the Russian economy have only stressed their dependence on it, and the zealous forcing out of the Russian-speaking population by pursuing discriminatory politics make the stability in the Baltic highly dependent on the balance of political forces within Russia. And finally, the outcome of economic and political transformations in the states of the former Soviet Union unequivocally depend on the fate of reforms in Russia. In the meanwhile, the "Russocentric" character of the post-Soviet environment is in no way revealed or promoted by the Russian leadership that does not take any actions aimed at reintegration.

Slavic States

The political situation in the **Slavic republics of the CIS (Ukraine and Belarus)**, notwithstanding their emphasized disunion with Moscow, is similar with that in Russia. The former nomenclatura majority in the parliaments and local authority bodies has retained its positions, but increasingly loses its political capacity. The anti-nomenclatura "democratic" opposition splits even before coming to power. The centrist forces of a moderate reformist kind gather momentum. The political scene is dominated by leaders of the state, the public profile of political parties is low, and the growing social discontent is accompanied by the political passivity of the population.

This scenario, however, is somewhat "delayed" in Ukraine and Belarus. The former Witold Fokin's Cabinet in Ukraine was attempting, and Vyacheslav Kebich's Cabinet in Belarus is still trying to implement the "Ryzhkov-type" economic reform. However, the new economic situation that was dramatically changed by the Russian reform, condemns such policies to failure. It was plainly shown by the recent fall of the Fokin Cabinet. Political barriers cannot impede the ties of the three republics that still remain "communicating vessels". By summer 1992 it has become evident that the break of economic ties with Russia means economic suicide for Belarus and Ukraine. This has resulted in Dagomys agreements of Boris Yeltsin and Leonid Kravtchuk and in signing the agreements between Russia and Belarus in July 1992.

In the meanwhile, anti-nomenclatura and "democratic" forces in Ukraine *("Rukh")* and Belarus (The Byelorussian Popular Front!) are, in contrast to Russia, nationalist-minded and patriotic-oriented. Given the close historical, cultural, and linguistic kinship of the three Slavic nations, the assertion of national identity of Ukrainians and Byelorussians especially Ukranians) will be taking place at the cost of cultural, linguistic and political disunion with Russia. Zealous effort is required to overcome the natural and genuine affinity of the Slavic nations. Hence the fervent patriotism and "Moskvophobia" of the Ukrainian and Byelorussian "national-democrats", seeking for an occasion to confront Russia (though in Belarus the positions of nationalists are much weaker than in Ukraine).

Apart from being economically devastating, such campaigns bring little political effect. 21 percent of the 52 million people living in Ukraine are Russians, and only one third of the country's population is actually speaking Ukrainian. That is why the national radicalism of *"Rukh"* can not win masses of supporters in Kiev, the Donetsk coal basin, Novorossia, the Crimea, and on the left-bank Ukraine in general. In other words, *"Rukh"* is confined to be a regional political force of the Western Ukraine, or, at its best, of the right-bank Ukraine. A shrewd politician like the President Leonid Kravtchuk had to realize the actual limits of nationalism. Having earned the reputation of a *"samostyinost"* (independence) champion in the first half of 1992, he later showed his other side that is of a pragmatic and flexible politician, free of "Moskvophobia", and able to maintain decent relations with Russia. Though the episodes of confrontation will be repeated, in the short- and medium-term perspectives Ukraine will be bound to a "pendulum movement" of approaching and moving away from Russia while staying on the "Moskvocentric" orbit. "The divorce with Russia" will stay a strategic priority of the Ukrainian politics, but the "divorce case" is going to be long and difficult.

As for Belarus, Russians comprise 12 percent of its population of 10 million. The linguistic russification went that far that proclaiming Byelorussian a state language did not add to its viability. In 1992, for instance, only 17 percent of Byelorussians were willing to have Byelorussian as a state language, compared to 25 percent in 1989. Only 6 percent of the native population favored teaching Byelorussian in schools in 1992, compared to 18 percent in 1989. The number of people using Byelorussian in everyday speech is five times smaller than in 1989.[32] There is no historic evidence to confrontation between Russians and Byelorussians and the Byelorussian national character is immune to extremism of any kind. Given this, the national radicalism of the Byelorussian Popular Front (BPF) did not win masses of supporters.

On the other side, the increase of social tension and the popular resentment against the nomenclatura-run parliament, allowed the BPF to collect the necessary number of signatures (450 thousand) in order to submit to the national referendum the issue of the extraordinary parliamentary elections. The opinion polls show, however, that the BPF could get no more than 11–13 percent of votes, the Communist Party 3–4.5 percent, and the remaining parties will get even less. From 62 to 73 percent of the questioned are politically undecided.[33] In the meanwhile, the centrist Chairman of the Presidium of the Supreme Soviet of Belarus Stanislav Shushkevitch maintained a 50 percent rating in the polls during 1992, by far surpassing his rivals. With political vacuum emerging, the most probable development is the transfer to a presidential republic with certain authoritarian features, in which democratic institutions will be formally functioning. Further developments will largely depend on the pace of events in Russia and Ukraine.

---

[32] Nezavisimaya Gazeta, 1992, September 1.
[33] Nezavisimaya Gazeta, 1992, June 5.

The Moldovian Conflict

The characteristic affinity with the situation in Russia, Ukraine and Belarus appeared also in **Rumanian-speaking Moldova**, where the Pridnestrovye-conflict created especially favorable conditions for a confrontation with Russia. Here, too, the post-totalitarian political system took shape of a neo-nomenclatura regime with authoritarian trends. The anti-nomenclatura "Popular Front" that barked on forced unification with Rumania, quickly exhausted its political resource and lost its appeal. The war in Pridnestrovye and the semi-loss of this strategic region,[34] the collapse of the Moldavian economy, mixed feelings about a unification with Rumania, even among native Moldavians which have uneasy memories about life in a Rumanian province in the interwar period, further weakened the opposition.

Further developments will be mostly determined by the course of settlement in Pridnestrovye. In case Moldavia reaches the compromise with Pridnestrovye, it will be bound to stay in the CIS milieu. This conforms to the interests of President Mircia Sneghur and the leaders of the neo-nomenclatura that could otherwise only hope to become provincial officials in Rumania. The independence of Moldova ensures the local elite economic and political dominance and balancing between Ukraine, Rumania, and Russia gives certain foreign policy advantages.

In case the armed conflict recommences, the unification of Moldavia and Rumania will be emerging as the only alternative. Russia and Ukraine will be facing hard choices concerning the future status of Pridnestrovye. Annexation by Russia of an outlying enclave will be a questionable acquisition and will set a dangerous precedent, posing a threat to the territorial integrity of Russia itself. In the meanwhile, the separation of Pridnestrovye and the possibility to use it as an instrument of pressure on Ukraine, Moldova, and Rumania might appear tempting for the Russian "state-minded" politicians. However, Russia has little legal rationale for such action.[35]

Ukraine has more formal reason to lay claim on Pridnestrovye that was part of its territory from 1924–1940. However, Kiev took a deliberately neutral and passive stand during the conflict. The recognition of a legitimate secession of Pridnestrovye as a result of the free ex-

---

[34] Pridnestrovye makes up 37 percent of the industrial potential of Moldavia, and produces 83 percent of electric power (Izvestiya, 1992, June 5).

[35] On the territory of Pridnestrovye live 39 percent Moldavians, 28 percent Ukrainians, 24 percent Russians, 9 percent Bulgarians, Gagauz, etc. (Nezavisimaya Gazeta, 1992, September 22). Out of 562,000 Russians living in Moldavia (that is 13 percent of the entire population) 75 percent live not in Pridnestrovye, but in the Right-Bank Moldavia (Izvestiya, 1992, June 9).

pression of the people's will could create a dangerous precedent for Ukraine itself, provoking similar actions in the Crimea, the Donetsk basin and in the Transcarpatian region. Most likely, Ukraine will favor the retention of a status quo in Pridnestrovye. A peaceful settlement of the conflict on the basis of Pridnestrovye's autonomy in the borders of Moldavia, as proposed earlier by President Leonid Kravtchuk, will remain a solution most suitable for Kiev.

The Transcaucasian Region

The situation in the **Transcaucasian region**, where nomenklatura regimes have been swept away, is essentially different. The only exception is the past of Azerbaijan, which is governed by the former republican Communist Party leader Geidar Aliev, the Nakhichevan Autonomous Republic.

The price of revolutionary changes has been high. With the "national-democratic" forces in office, the existent ethnic tensions quickly developed into full-fledged military conflicts. The internal stability has been ruined, and this overshadows the prospects for economic development. The situation could be favorable for market reforms, but the militarized economy retains its administrative character. Beside this, none of the three republics has an elaborate program of market transition, or the necessary conditions (investment, trained personnel, etc.). In the Transcaucasian region, Armenia has better chances for economic reform, where land has already been turned into private property, and the rich and educated Armenian diaspora could give a start to reform in case peace is established. But the country is progressively ruined by the war.

The war in Georgia between separatist Abkhazians and the Tbilisi government is delivering a coup de grace to the already devastated economy of this formerly prosperous and market oriented country.

While the democratic procedures have been formally introduced in Azerbaijan, Georgia, and Armenia, the actual political life in the Transcaucasian republics is determined by the balance of forces between armed units. With armed conflicts expanding, the army and law enforcement authorities emerge as key actors on the political scene. As to the conflicts themselves, they can be stopped either by external pressure, or by full exhaustion of both conflicting parties. It is thus evident that authoritarian trends will be getting the upper hand in the post-totalitarian society, no matter whether there are neo-nomenklatura or anti-nomenklatura forces in office.

The Central Asian Republics

The developments in the **Central Asian republics** of the CIS ranged from setting up neo-nomenclatura regimes to anti-nomenclatura revolutions (Tajikistan). The crash of communism has only removed the upper ideological veil that was covering the traditional oriental hierarchical power structure. Conventional wisdom of European residents of the USSR has always held that "there is no Soviet Power in Central Asia", i.e. that the Soviet legislation and party regulations were actually not effective there. Quite as superficial was the implantation of Western democratic institutions in this traditional Asian society that has fully retained its feudal and tribal structure.

Given ethnic tensions in the region, further complicated by tribal and clannish contradictions, the only guarantee of political stability is the conservation of neo-nomenclatura regimes of two basic kinds: a "soft" authoritarian regime, inclined to economic reforms, with a relatively free press and multiparty democracy (Nursultan Nazarbayev in Kazakhstan, and Askar Akayev in Kirghizstan) and a "hard" authoritarian regime with a heavy censorship on the press, a token opposition, and obscure perspectives for economic reform (Sapurmurad Niyazov in Turkmenistan and Islam Karimov in Uzbekistan). The fall of these regimes will inevitably lead to civil war and ethnic armed conflicts of the Afghan type, as clearly shown by the recent upheaval in Tajikistan.

As a first sign of such developments a massive exodus of the Russian-speaking population will start.[36] This runs the danger of further internal destabilization in Russia and cultural and economic degradation in Central Asia. Given the ethnic composition of the industrial working class, scientific, and technical personnel in these republics, the withdrawal of Caucasians will simply mean a deindustrialization. Notwithstanding the growing presence of Islam in everyday life in Uzbekistan and Tajikistan, and to a lesser degree in Kazakhstan, Kirghizstan and Turkmenistan, it could win as a political force only in case of the general regional upheaval in Central Asia, before which time the processes of state, national, regional, ethnic, tribal, and clannish differentiation will prevail.

---

[36] According to the 1989 census, among Uzbekistan's 20 million population, 11 percent were Russian-speaking; compared to 10 percent in 5 million population in Tajikistan; 22 percent in 4 million population in Kirghizstan; and 13 percent in 4 million population in Turkmenistan (Moskovskiye Novosti [The Moscow News], 1991, No 40, October 6, p. 9). Due to instability in Tajikistan in 1990–1991, over 70 thousand Russians left the republic before the outbreak of the civil war, and by spring 1992 the total number of Russians went down to 300,000 (5.5 percent of the population) (Nezavisimaya Gazeta, 1992, June 9).

Due to the intricate ethnic structure of the Central Asian states and the artificial character of borders between them, local conflicts in any of the republics can easily spread across the borders and become the hotbed of instability for the entire region. Thus the civil war in Tajikistan has directly affected the Uzbek population (1.2 million people, or 23 percent of the population of Tajikistan), especially in the Leninabad Oblast, evoking repercussions in Uzbekistan. Still unclear is the orientation of the Tajik population of Bukhara and Samarkand (4.7 percent of the population of Uzbekistan). The 1991 massacre in Osh has already revealed the potential for ethnic conflicts between Uzbeks and Kirghizs. In the meanwhile, 550 thousand Uzbeks make up 12.9 percent of the population of Kirghizstan. Lack of arable land and water as well as overpopulation will permanently be giving rise to conflicts even in a relatively stable environment. From this point of view, the most risky and unstable area is the rich and fertile Ferghana valley, where the borders of Uzbekistan, Kirghizstan and Tajikistan meet, and where three murderous ethnic conflicts already took place over the recent years.

Civil wars in Tajikistan and the neighboring Afghanistan (where 4,2 million Tajiks and 1.8 million Uzbeks live)[37] made the southern border of the CIS, controlled by the Russian troops, extremely vulnerable and bluntly questioned the stability and the very existence of the Central Asian regimes. This was well realized by the Central Asian leaders. As Islam Karimov put it, "We understand quite well that without reliance on Russia's potential we, as well as our neighbors, can hardly outline the perspective and find the way out of the present deep crisis. We see Russia's role as that of an advocate of peace and stability, the guarantor of inviolability of our external frontiers".[38]

The reliance on Russia, however, has nothing to do with the prospects of economic reform in Central Asian republics. The only exception could be Turkmenistan, where a relatively small population of 4 million and vast resources of oil and gas resemble the situation in the oil emirates of the Gulf some 30 years ago and could provide for an economic boost. Such a model could be tempting for the rest, but is absolutely irrelevant for the poor Kirghizstan, and for the overpopulated Uzbekistan.

The opposition in Central Asian republics, too, does not favor market reforms. At this point, the national theme interferes in the econ-

---

[37] S. I. BRUK Narody SSSR v strane i za rubezhom (Peoples of the USSR in the Country and Abroad). – Moscow, 1991, pp. 25–26.
[38] Nezavisimaya Gazeta, 1992, June 2.

omy. For instance, the Republican Party of Kazakhstan (the organization of moderate nationalists) and the *"Alash"* Pan-Turkic and fundamentalist movement stand against privatization and foreign participation in exploiting mineral resources, because "the Kazakh population is not yet ready to live under the market", and "will not take a proper part in this process"[39]. In Kirghizstan, too, the national-democratic organizations like *"Erkin Kirghizstan"* and *"Asaba"* fight against auctions as a means of privatization, because poor competitiveness of Kirghizs excludes them from the sphere of private enterprise.[40] The land reform in Kirghizstan also meets great difficulties, because the most fertile land in the Ferghana Valley is populated by Uzbeks and Tajiks, and in the Chuisk Valley by Russians, Ukrainians and Germans. Thus the privatization in industry and agriculture in all Central Asian republics will permanently be overrun by ethnic problems.

Taken *per se,* out of the post-Soviet political context, the Central Asian republics could be moving towards state capitalism of the African type, with elements of foreign investment, and private enterprise in agriculture, retail trade and handicraft. Political life will then be mostly determined by competition of tribal, criminal, drug business, and groups with frequent military coups.

On the other hand, such a scenario appears rather hypothetical. The impossibility of reaching political balance without the Russian engagement, along with grave consequences of the economic break with Russia have given rise to reintegration trends in the region, and at least three countries – Kazakhstan, Kirghizstan, and Uzbekistan – are inclined to closer cooperation in the framework of the CIS.

---

[39] Nezavisimaya Gazeta, 1992, April 11, June 2.
[40] Nezavisimaya Gazeta, 1992, March 10.

7. Interstate Relations in Post-Soviet Politics

The New Power Constellation

The systematic crisis that predetermined the breakup of the Soviet Union is not only maintained in the post-Soviet period, but actually questions the very existence of the new independent states by pushing them to the same disintegration that was characteristic of the Soviet Union in its late years. Ethnic conflicts and increased tensions in interstate relations (between Russia and Estonia, Armenia and Azerbaijan) are underlaid by political, economic, and cultural crises that destroy the emerging identity of the new states on the territory of the former USSR.

Some stabilization could certainly be reached by reintegration.[41] The potential of reintegration, however, is heavily restrained by at least four obstacles (some of these are treated in chapter 2). Firstly, the deepening economic crisis[42] compels the governments of the new independent states to protect their internal markets. Secondly, the new national political elites[43] have an objective interest in maintaining the trend of disintegration in order to consolidate their regimes. Thirdly, the leaders in the former Soviet republics constantly face the danger of disintegration of their own states and of general instability. And fourthly, all new independent states overtly favor relations with the countries beyond the post-Soviet political scene.

---

[41] See: Yuri BORKO, Vporu li Sodruzhestvu uroki Soobshestva? (Does the Experience of the Community fit the Commonwealth?) // Svobodnaya Mysl (The Free Thought), 1992, No 12, 65 p.

[42] On the economic situation in the post-Soviet world, See: Ç. ILLARIONOV, Byvshie sovetskiye respubliki v mirovoy systeme economicheskykh coordinat (The Former Soviet Republics in the World Economic Setup) // Voprosy Economiky (The Questions of Economics), 1992, No 4–6, 122 p.

[43] The study of the national elites of the former Soviet Union has just started. See: Iikhail MALYUTIN, "Novaya" elita v novoi Rossii (The New Elite in the New Russia) // Obshestvennye Nauki i Sovremennost (Social Sciences and the Contemporary World), 1992, No 2, 36 p.

It is quite apparent that the key role in the future developments in the region belongs to the Russian Federation. It was Russia that made the breakup of the Soviet Union irreversible. It was the Russian Federation that in certain cases almost imposed independence on some of the Soviet Republics. The geographical position facilitates the presence of Russia in all key areas of the former USSR. The population of 150 million, the economic potential, the role of Russia (even given the current decline in oil production) as one of the leading suppliers of oil and gas for the former Soviet Republics, and finally, the presence of 28 million Russians beyond the borders of the Russian Federation[44] make Russia a predominant force in this part of Eurasia. The success or failure of the economic reform and the democratic process in Russia will inevitably provoke a chain reaction that will largely determine developments in most parts of the former Soviet Republics.

An Alliance for the Future of the CIS

The Russian Federation will hardly be able to maintain a fair level of political stability on the territory of the former Soviet Union without a close alliance and support of Belarus and Kazakhstan. The relations among these three states will to a large extent stay the same. Both Belarus and Kazakhstan largely depend on Russia in the economic domain. In the foreseeable future they will continue to bark on cooperation with Russia in political, economic, military, and cultural fields.[45]

This has certain geopolitical repercussions. Together with Belarus Russia will be able to maintain geopolitical pressure in such important a region as the Baltic. That same Belarus may be considered a geographical link between Russia and Europe.

The Russian-Ukrainian relations will most likely take a different turn. Despite the obvious interdependence of the two states, including that in economics, Kiev regards integration as a direct threat to the Ukrainian independence. In the foreseeable future Kiev will be laying emphasis on keeping away from Moscow in the political sphere.[46] The notorious disputes about the Black Sea fleet, the Cri-

---

[44] See: Sergei STANKEVICH, Derzhava v poiskakh sebya (The Power Looking for its Place) // Nezavisimaya Gazeta, 1992, March 28, p. 5.
[45] See: Vitaly PORTNIKOV, Rossia i Belorussia sozdayut novy Soyuz? (Do Russia and Belarus Create a New Union?) // Nezavisimaya Gazeta, 1992, July 22, p. 1.
[46] Alexander LIKHOTAL, The New Russia and Eurasia // Security Dialogue, 1992, Vol. 23, No 3, p. 15.

mea, and the nuclear arms on the territory of Ukraine appear more like a prelude to future controversies than disagreements inherited from the past.

Given the present trends of the Russian-Ukrainian relations, it will not be the specific economic and political divisions that matter, but the general rivalry between the two Slavic powers. From this point of view, the political priorities and the kind of economic regime in Russia and Ukraine are of little importance for the future of their relations, as the context of rivalry will be present in all variations of their future development.

Oscillating between rivalry and cooperation, the relations between Moscow and Kiev can be evolving along different lines. The most optimistic scenario holds that Russia and Ukraine will finally realize that it does not pay to swing the boat in which both of them are. In that case, at least until the statehood of both countries is finally established and the economic and political stability is reached, they will see in each other partners rather than rivals.

The variant of the moderate Russian-Ukrainian rivalry holds that mutual distrust will remain at the present level. Ukraine will be accusing Moscow of imperial ambitions, and Russia will find numerous occasions to reproach Kiev on "uncivilized behavior". The rivalry will hardly go beyond this moderate level, chiefly because domestic problems will not let Kiev challenge Moscow on the post-Soviet political scene.

It is quite possible though, that for a number of reasons Kiev will turn to a clear-cut anti-Russian policy in the nearest future, thus trying to satisfy its ambitions and to divert attention of the population from economic hardships.[47] Protracted rivalry between Moscow and Kiev assumes that geopolitical interests will be put into the forefront. Ukraine will certainly try to play on its geographical position between Russia and Europe. To cover this card, Moscow could try to bark on relations with Minsk, partly isolating Ukraine and gaining access to North and Central Europe. Thus the sharpened Russian-Ukrainian rivalry will be largely focussed on the problem of interaction with the West.[48]

---

[47] Different alternatives for the Russian-Ukrainian relations are treated in the article of Dmitry FADEYEV in the journal "Yevropa i Mir" (Europe and the World) (No 3, forthcoming). The views of the Ukrainian analyst Igor KHARTCHENKO on the future of the Russian-Ukrainian relations (comparative models: USA-Canada, USSR-Finland, USSR-Austria, USSR-Poland in the 20s, the Yugoslavian model) are treated in: Yuri LEONOV, Rossia i Ukraina posle gibeli SNG (Russia and Ukraine after the breakup of the CIS) // Nezavisimaya Gazeta, 1992, April 18, p. 2.

[48] This trend is already perceptible. See: Sergei GUK, Ukraina prosit NATO okazat' nazhim na Rossiyu (Ukraine asks NATO to apply pressure on Russia) // Izvestiya, 1992, June 5, p. 1.

The aggravation of the Russian-Ukrainian relations will inevitably pose the problem of over 11 million Russians living in Ukraine. These people and several millions of only Russian-speaking Ukrainians will be strongly opposed to the deepening of the rift.[49] Such a hypothetical development runs the danger of disintegrating Ukraine into three or four states.

Ethno-Cultural Dangers on the Borders of the Russian Federation

The most explosive regional situation is that in the Caucasus and Central Asia. The immediate impact of the Caucasian region on the former Soviet Union will be predictably higher as it will be spreading through Russia that occupies a dominant position on the post-Soviet political scene. As a matter of fact, the war between Armenia and Azerbaijan and ethnic conflicts in Georgia have only marked the beginning of the period of permanent instability. The fragile political and ethnic balance in the northern Caucasus and the Transcaucasian region that existed until recently has been created for decades and now is being swiftly destroyed. A single outbreak in a small district may cause the "domino effect" that will completely undermine stability in the entire region. Beside this, the ambitions of Russia in this region are so vague and unexplicit that it is hard to predict the future evolution of Russian policies.

In the years to come Moscow will be much more concerned with the situation in the northern Caucasus, rather than by the Transcaucasian region. It is the Northern Caucasus that appears to be a geopolitical bomb for the Russian Federation. It is now quite apparent that the northern Caucasian republics no longer depend on Moscow. Beside this, the political situation in the region is so intricate that the local power will most probably remain unstable.

It is quite possible that the approach of a part of the northern Caucasian nations to Russia will be strongly motivated by an anti-Russian sentiment. A substantial part of the region's population will most likely consider Turkey as a possible key partner. This alternative, though, will hardly provide for stability in all of the Caucasus regions. One can anticipate that the growth of Turkish influence will provoke a pro-Russian reaction, in particular among the Georgian and Armenian population. It will most probably be Georgia and Ar-

---

[49] According to some researchers, most part of the East Ukrainians was "russified" and will hardly take an explicit anti-Russian stand. See: David LATIN. The National Uprising in the Soviet Union // World Politics, 1991, October, No 44, pp. 159–161.

menia, the countries with a relatively small percentage of Russian population, who will show most interest in Russia's return to the Transcaucasian region.[50]

Another potentially explosive region is Central Asia and Kazakhstan.[51] The states of this region strongly depend on Russia in the economic field. The current trends indicate, however, that Moscow is going to take a rather cautious approach to developments in Central Asia. Another potential regional hegemon, Kazakhstan is also not willing to engage in settling conflicts on the territory of his southern neighbors. It is quite evident, though, that it is precisely the role of mediator and peacekeeper that will determine the status of the powers in Central Asia.[52]

It is also evident that several "out-of-the CIS-area" international actors are concurrently expanding their influence in the region. Turkey, Iran, Saudi Arabia, Pakistan, Afghanistan, India and the USA have already claimed a stake in Central Asia.[53] All the more in case of a Russian withdrawal from the region, the power vacuum will not be filled *tout de suite*. It is growingly clear for the leaders of the Central Asian republics that while they can get some moral and economic help from their southern partners, they cannot rely on them for the help they really need: a propping up of their regimes. There is also little hope that the concurrent presence of so many different political forces will bolster regional stability.

Russia's Role in the Interstate Relations of the CIS Member States

The interstate relations on the post-Soviet political scene will thus be characterized by two main features: direct or indirect domination of Russia (this depends on its strategy and ad hoc approaches) and the presence of a conflict potential. The principal correlation between

---

[50] Georgia and Armenia have always had the lowest percentage of the Russian population among the republics of the Soviet Union. See: Emil PAIN, Gde russkiye zhivut kak doma? (Where do Russians feel at home?) // Nezavisimaya Gazeta, 1992, July 31, p. 5.

[51] On the situation in the Central Asia, See: Nikolai ANDREYEV, Srednyaya Aziya bez Moskvy (The Central Asia without Moscow) // Izvestiya, 1992, June 24, p. 3; Ç. SHUMILIN, Islamsky peredel (The Islamic redivision) // Komsomolskaya pravda, 1992, January 14, p. 2; D. SABOV, I. CHERNYAK, Russkiye na fone mechetei (Russians against the background of Mosques // Komsomolskaya pravda, 1992, February 4, p. 2.

[52] The politics of Russia in the Central Asian region is treated in detail in: Sergei KARAGANOV, Russia and Other Independent Republics in Asia // Paper delivered at the IISS Annual Conference, September 1992, Seoul.

[53] See: Vladimir KHOVRATOVITCH, Bor'ba za sovetskiye musulmanskiye respubliki obostryaetsya (The struggle for the Soviet Islamic republics gets sharper) // Izvestiya, 1991, December 9, p. 3.

these two elements will determine the degree of political stability in each region of the former Soviet Union. For instance the withdrawal of Russia from Central Asia and the Caucasus will result in extreme instability and unpredictability of the situation, while the dynamic presence of Russia in both of these regions will make the interstate relations more manageable.

In any case, Moscow will hardly be able to adhere to some pure course. For instance the activity of the "Transcaucasian lobby" in high echelons of power in Moscow will constrain the idea of Russia's withdrawal from the Caucasus, and the existence of a large Ukrainian diaspora in Russia limits the freedom of maneuver for Moscow in case of a conflict with Ukraine. Both are in the mood of keeping away from existing or potential conflicts and have recurrent desire to engage in events on the territory of the former Soviet Union.

8. The CIS: a Year After

First Results

Though the emergence of the Commonwealth of Independent States in December 1991 as a result of the agreement of the three Slavic republics (Russia, Ukraine and Belarus) marks the beginning of the new political era, it is deeply rooted in the preceding Gorbachev epoch. It needs to be examined in the framework of the political evolution of the USSR in the years 1985–1991. This development completed the long process of decay of the Soviet statehood and cast the final blow on the entire system of political power of the USSR, already shaken by the so-called coup in August 1991 and on Mikhail Gorbachev's regime. There was less than a month left for the President of the USSR to lay down the remains of the authority he possessed.

Paradoxical as it may sound, preconditions for the emergence of the CIS were contained in the Gorbachevian perestroika itself. Conceived as a broad and idealistic project of reforming socialism and integrating it into the world community, perestroika did not really possess any positive recipes or an integral conception of reforms. It simply envisaged the liberation of some social forces that were supposed to harmoniously join the course of reforms under the general guidance of the Communist Party. There was little harmony, though. Those social forces, deformed by decades of constraint, bore an enormous potential of destruction and once unleashed, quickly started to get out of centralized control. Beginning about 1987–1988, the processes of disintegration in the society, the state structure, on the ethnic and regional level, and in the mass consciousness gained momentum. Apart from the intentions of the forefathers of perestroika, destruction became its main theme. The years 1989–1991 were already dominated by the inertia of destruction.

Based on unofficial evidence and information leaks, the idea of destroying the USSR by forming an alternative Union without a center goes back to late 1990 or early 1991, and was put forward by the Ukrainian leader Leonid Kravtchuk and/or some individuals from Boris Yeltsin's team. The Novo-Ogarevo process under the auspices of Gorbachev started in spring 1991 with the purpose of signing the new Union Treaty, but parallel to it developed another process of separate talks in the triangle Russia-Ukraine-Belarus, with the possible addition of Kazakhstan. The idea of the Union without a center and without a political rival like Gorbachev looked very appealing to the leaders of the three Slavic republics with the largest economic and human potential in the USSR. They saw it as the easiest way to strengthen and upgrade their political positions, i.e. to establish their individual regimes at the head of fully independent states.

August 1991, while explicitly discrediting the center and Gorbachev gave a dramatic boost to this process. The destructive trend associated with perestroika entered its final stage. In early December Boris Yeltsin, Stanislav Shushkevitch, and Leonid Kravtchuk, who had just been elected President of Ukraine and had finally legitimated his power, entered into a hasty, private, and legally questionable agreement founding the Commonwealth of Independent States. It is highly probable that some Russian participants (most probably not B.Yeltsin), L. Kravtchuk, and possibly S. Shushkevitch regarded the CIS at the time merely as an instrument of disintegration, an institutional framework for the so-called "civilized divorce". Otherwise they would not have kept the Kazakh President Nursultan Nazarbayev, opposed to such a radical breakup of the old Union, out of the agreement.

The game was made. The CIS, a finished product of the Soviet period, a child of perestroika, found itself in a post-Soviet, post-perestroika environment. In the first weeks of 1992 there was little doubt about its soon and inevitable death. The death, however, did not follow. In the meanwhile, the situation has rapidly deteriorated. The ethnic conflicts escalated, economic disbalances and the breakup of traditional links led to a dramatic fall in production, discords on political and military matters, including the division of the Army, Navy and nuclear weapons, added to each other, the refugees started to flood certain areas of the country, and the specter of the Hobbsian "war of all against all" emerged. These were not the politicians, rather the atmosphere itself that brought about the necessity to hold up these uncontrolled developments. That is how the striking metamorphosis started: the CIS, born for disintegration, gradually, to a certain extent unconsciously and unexpectedly for some of its founders, began to evolve into the instrument for deterring disintegration.

The dangerous post-Soviet contingencies altered the functions of the Commonwealth.

It is certainly premature to talk of any reintegrative trends (though the potential for re-integration exists). The CIS is no more than a means for slowing down disintegration. It is not even a form of statehood or inter-state organization on the territory of the former Soviet Union. This is a vague and fairly conditional formula, rather a symbol. But as a matter of fact, politics are made up mostly of symbols and myths. The symbol of the CIS indicates and emphasizes an actual, not mythical community of interests of tens of millions of people on the territory of the former USSR, stresses the cohesion of its constituent parts, and also gives an opportunity to search for a new and still unclear future framework of cooperation and possible reintegration.

Summary

Summing up the results of the first year of the CIS, it is necessary to stress the main achievement: despite the momentum of the centrifugal forces, the Commonwealth survived. Notwithstanding all failures and growing-pains, it endured to become a political reality on the territory of the former Soviet Union and in the international scope. This main positive accomplishment enables us to better assess the specific results.

An important political and psychological breakthrough is wident: the countries of the CIS started to overcome the inertia of alienation born by the old Union and inherited by the Commonwealth. It has become clear that the doubts of winter and spring of 1992 about its viability were premature. Such institutions as the Council of Heads of States and the Council of Heads of Governments proved to be fairly effective instruments of coordinating various approaches and working out a joint stand.

In the meanwhile, the countries of the CIS came to an agreement or stated joint approaches in such fields as transport, energy, price formation, the functioning of the rouble zone, environment protection, social security, the transparency of frontiers, and customs tariffs. The questions of the succession of the USSR in international organizations and of the division of the Soviet external debt were settled. The military problems were usually solved without sharp disagreements. The order of implementing the START and CFE Treaties was agreed on. Despite the repeated surges of ambitions among the "nuclear" states of the CIS, the problem of control over the Soviet nuclear potential is clearly solvable in general. Nine states of the Commonwealth signed a Treaty on Collective Security in Tashkent in May 1992, and thus a potential CIS military nucleus is emerging. By developing special mechanisms and starting to implement them, the CIS proved capable if not to solve, at least to react to regional conflicts. The parliamentary assembly along the lines of the European Parliament has been established. The most recent question on the agenda is the establishment of the Common Bank of the CIS.

Finally, the CIS is quickly evolving on institutional, structural lines. The Working Group for preparing sessions of the Council of Heads of States and the Council of Heads of Governments has been created, the Statute and Regulations of Procedure for both Councils have been adopted. Also working are the Council of Foreign Ministers, the Council of Defense Ministers, and a number of councils and committees for different fields and branches of economy. The agenda for the sessions of the Council of Heads of States is fine tuned at the meetings of the Council of Foreign Ministers, while the sessions of the Council of Heads of Governments are preceded by meetings of appropriate ministers.

What is probably most important is that there are preconditions for creating a large bureaucracy on all levels of power deeply rooted in the structures of the CIS. The experience of the European Community demonstrates that the institutional interests of this bureaucracy have an important stabilizing and integrating effect. That means that in the current uncertain phase of the evolution of the CIS this newborn bureaucracy in numerous embassies, delegations, commissions, in the Commonwealth Department in the Russian Foreign Ministry (at present the idea of setting up a separate Ministry for the Commonwealth Affairs is being studied in Russia) has a good chance to play a helpful role.

It was clear that the configuration of the CIS would be asymmetrical even before it emerged, and life gave proof to this. Two groups of states have taken shape inside the CIS: seven of them (Russia, Belarus, Kazakhstan, Armenia, Kirghizstan, Tajikistan, and recently Uzbekistan) are inclined to closer cooperation on a multilateral basis, and the other four (Ukraine, Moldova, Azerbaijan, and Turkmenistan) take a somewhat more separate stand. In the meanwhile, Ukraine and Turkmenistan begin to join multilateral cooperation in certain fields, and Moldova and Azerbaijan that have not yet ratified the agreement of the formation of the CIS are seeking to more actively participate in joint programs.

The possibility of Georgia joining the CIS is a separate topic. The return of Eduard Shevardnadze to Georgia shows a definite interest in developing bilateral relations with Russia and multilateral relations with the countries of the Commonwealth. At present this process of reintegrating Georgia into the broader political milieu after the Zviad Gamsakhurdia autarky and self-imposed isolation is blocked by the instability of the Shevardnadze regime, its concentration on domestic problems, by the military conflicts in South Ossetia, West Georgia, and especially by the war in Abkhazia. However, the possibilities for rapprochement of Georgia with the CIS stay more or less intact. The same conflict potential in the western part of the republic and a clear and present danger of a major Caucasian war against Georgia may pressure Tbilisi to seek political settlement of conflicts in the framework of multilateral agreement, and actually in the framework of the CIS.

Beside this, much has been done in the field of bilateral relations between the subjects of the CIS, and this is certainly not to be missed. General political treaties are being concluded between the republics, and thus the axes are being formed that support the complex and shaky structure of the CIS. The most important of those are Russia-Belarus and Russia-Kazakhstan. Several successful bilateral summits, like the Russian-Ukrainian in the Crimea and the Russian-Moldavian in Moscow are also not to be disregarded.

The possibilities of the CIS are far from being exhausted. It is yet difficult to imagine them in full. From a mere symbol, a formula of possible coexistence of nations, the CIS may grow into a real political force. It is still one of many currents in a stormy ocean of post-Soviet politics, and not a main one. Parallel to it are two other trends, much more radical and explosive: one towards complete disintegration and so-called regionalization, and an imperial trend. The Commonwealth is simultaneously affected by various integrative impulses coming, for example, from the part of the Russian political establishment ("The Civic Union" and some other parties), from the Kazakh President Nursultan Nazarbayev or the Kirghiz President Askar Akayev, etc., and by anti-integrational impulses from, say, Kiev or Kishinev. The future of the post-Soviet world largely depends on whether this trend associated with the Commonwealth will prevail and become an initiatory and productive one. This is important for the global development as well, for the CIS may be seen as one of the ways for seeking a new paradigm of cooperation between north and south, a contemporary model of multinational coexistence.

9. The Alternative Scenarios

The general political situation in the Commonwealth of Independent States will be determined in a decisive way by the state of affairs in Russia, its foreign policy, especially towards the countries of the CIS.

Another crucial factor is the state of relations between the largest countries of the CIS: Russia, Ukraine, Belarus and Kazakhstan. In the last months Russia and Ukraine managed to reduce tensions in their bilateral relations, to bring the contradictions among them under a certain level of control. Nevertheless, the outcomes of the summit of leaders of the CIS countries which took place in Bishkek on October 9, 1992, showed again that Ukraine continues to object strongly to a creation of structures within the CIS for coordinating and implementing the CIS decisions.

The events of recent months (a sharpening of the problem of resettlement of the Crimean Tatars, the extremely poor state of the economy) give grounds for conclusions that trends towards a destabilization of the domestic situation in Ukraine gain momentum, and a further worsening of the domestic crisis is a reality. This might stimulate a domestic struggle in Ukraine and might strengthen the positions of radical political groupings which call for a withdrawal of the country from the CIS and for a hostile relationship with Russia.

Another important factor is the probable dynamic evolving from the CIS, the correlation of trends towards disintegration and reintegration. As was shown in preceding chapters, the trend towards disintegration on the territory of the former USSR is still prevailing. The number of the CIS countries is decreasing. The parliament of Azerbaijan recently did not ratify the Alma-Ata Treaties on the creation of the CIS, and now it is possible to consider this republic either as an observer or an associated member of the CIS, if provisions for such an affiliation are put into the final draft of the CIS Charter, being discussed now. The Parliament of Moldova also did not yet approve these treaties.

But since the summer of 1992, the trend towards reintegration started to get momentum. For the first time since the creation of the Commonwealth, specific ideas on strengthening the CIS, and creating some coordinating bodies appeared (N. Nazarbayev's initiatives). Another important new development is the formation of organizations of industrialists and businessmen, in all major CIS countries (Russia, Ukraine, Belarus, and Kazakhstan) calling for restoration of the broken trade, economic, and financial ties between the former republics of the USSR. The new trend towards reintegration reflects the already reached level of international recognition of all countries of the CIS; the emergence of real possibilities to pursue independent foreign policies for all of them; the widening understanding that consequences of disintegration of the USSR are becoming more and more dangerous; the increased need of many republics for broader cooperation with Russia, and among themselves.

One has to note that the new prime minister of Ukraine L. Kuchma recognized that "the restoration of all ties with Russia is one of the most important tasks" of his cabinet.

But all in all, the existence of the CIS and of Russia as an independent state is too short to make far reaching conclusions about their future. Uncertainty and instability in Russia and the CIS are still so high that it is possible only to consider different alternatives of developments, to describe contingencies and trends, which influence the probability of these alternatives.

Russian Scenarios

While evaluating alternatives of Russia's future in the near perspective, it is necessary to stress two important circumstances.

Firstly, the continuation of present trends in the domestic life of the country (low effectiveness of economic reforms, deep economic crisis, increase of social differentiation, continuing slow disintegration of Russia, etc.) becomes practically impossible, and furthermore, even dangerous.

The majority of Russian politicians, experts, and businessmen consider that this situation could continue only until the end of this year, or as maximum, until the spring of 1993. Even the Russian President Boris Yeltsin recently had to agree to this point of view.

Secondly, the Russian society is entering a new phase of political struggle on all major issues of its domestic and foreign policy, especially economic reforms that will in many regards be decisive for the destiny of the country in the near future.

If corrections of the economic course will not be made during the forthcoming months to slow down the dramatic decrease of industrial production, and if the confrontation between the government and the parliament will not be put under control, the replacement of the present regime by non-democratic means may become almost inevitable.

It is possible to consider the following major scenarios of development of the internal situation in Russia:

Scenario No 1: the centrist-conservative alternative. The driving force of this alternative is the bloc of parties of moderate and centrist orientation, which formed the well-known "Civic Union" (A. Volsky, A. Rutskoi, N. Travkin, A. Vladislavlev, V. Lipitsky and others). Today this bloc may be the most authoritative political force in the Russian society. The "Civic Union" has relatively well-known, popular leaders and comparatively elaborated concepts for further economic reforms, the future of Russia, its place and role in the world community. The "Union" comprises pragmatically oriented politicians, directors of state enterprises, some businessmen, many representatives of the military-industrial complex, and a certain part of engineers, technicians and people from academic circles. The "Civic Union" calls for continuing, economic reforms, but at a slower pace; for persistent implementation of the principle of the division of powers; for strengthening federal authorities in the political system of Russia; and for a broader integration within the CIS. As far as foreign politics are concerned, the Western orientation is maintained, but with more critical overtones. Larger emphasis is laid on relations with some Asian countries, first of all with China, South Korea, and Turkey.

This political bloc, at least so far, did not openly proclaim that coming to power is the main purpose of its activity and preferred to wage a dialogue with the Government on problems of continuing economic reform, stressing that the strategic choice made by the Government in this sphere, is justified. However, the "Civic Union" could come to power by means of the so-called "quiet coup", that is by gradually taking crucial governmental posts without seeking for resignation of the Russian President Boris Yeltsin. Anyway, such a resignation is not the goal of the bloc.

Nevertheless, under certain circumstances the "Civic Union" may conclude that a tactical cooperation, at least for the time being, with "The United Opposition" is justifiable (see the next scenario). Slogans of restoration of the Russian statehood as the only political instrument for consolidation of the Russian nation at the present historical moment, as well as calls for introducing extraordinary measures to prevent the collapse of the economy are supported by certain leaders of the "Civic Union". Such ideas may bear seeds of possible transformation of the centrist-conservative scenario into some kind of conservative-nationalistic authoritarianism.

A reasonable compromise between the government and the moderate centrist political forces might become an optimal tactical way out of the present tense and complicated situation in Russia, which would permit to continue economic reforms with less painful consequences for the society, to isolate reactionary forces, and by these means, to prevent a gigantic catastrophe. However, the partial neo-conservative stabilization will not solve the basic social and economic problems. Most probably it will have to be followed by a new wave of liberal reforms, but in a more controlled environment, which should be created by semi-authoritarian technocrats of the "Civic Union". However, if the new neo-conservative leadership, which will almost inevitably come to power within the next year, proves to be unable to strengthen the government, to stop the process of disintegration of Russia, and to curtail corruption, and inflation, it could be swept away by social unrest, which could be saddled by the "red-brown" opposition.

Scenario No 2: the red-brown alternative, i.e. the coming to power of "The United Opposition" in conditions of rising popular discontent with the governmental policies. The opposition bloc consists of such parties, movements and organizations as "the Russian Nationwide Union" (S. Baburin, N. Pavlov); "the Russian National" *Sobor* (Council) (A. Sterligov, V. Rasputin); "the Constitutional Democratic Party" (M. Astafiev); "the Russian Christian Democratic Movement" (V. Aksiuchits), and of a number of neo-communist parties and groups (chapter 5).

"The United Opposition" rejects any idea about correcting the present course of economic reforms. According to their views, these reforms have completely failed, and the only way to stop further deepening of the economic crisis is the development of a special program of anti-crisis measures. The opposition actively pursues its other key ideas: the greatness of Russia (often it implies the former Soviet Union), unlawfulness of the dissolution of the Soviet Union and of the CIS, the restoration of the Union in the old form, Pan-Slavic ideas, patriotism in traditional Russian spirit, the stopping of a humiliation of the Russian people in Russia, and in other countries as well, and finally, the total opposition to Yeltsin's government, including an already expressed readiness to demand the resignation of the President of Russia.

"National patriots" still view global developments as a continuation of confrontation of Russia with a hostile international environment, where Russia is currently being defeated and consider any weakening of military strength as a national betrayal. "The United Opposition" has already started to form the structures of the so-called "National Salvation Front" on central and local levels, considering them to be major instruments of political struggle (these were banned by President Boris Yeltsin in late October 1992.) This Front according to the plans of the opposition should replace the present regime in Russia.

The analysis of the worst possible scenarios of development of the situation in Russia, undertaken by Russian scholars in the summer of 1992 (nine-point scale was used), showed that the probability of coming to power of the opposition was equal to six points. Other research, though, gave proof that only 10 percent of the population in Russia supported the ideas of right-wing politicians. In spite of a certain dramatization of the red-brown threat, it would be a serious risk to underestimate this danger. This risk could become a reality not in the coming months or a year but later, provided the government proves incapable to slow down the decline in living standards (especially in food consumption) in major industrial centers and in the two Russian capitals, and to compensate for unemployment and shortages by massive privatization and support of small businesses. This is the key factor in preventing the reactionaries from coming to power, and in preventing the disintegration of Russia. In order to prevent this, crucial measures must be taken in the coming months in delegating powers to the regions and in putting barriers to further political disintegration.

Instead of saving Russia, the coming to power of the opposition will result in a new catastrophic international isolation of the country, in a sharpening of internal conflicts, and even in civil wars and conflicts with neighbors. However, this regime will most probably try to concentrate on suppressing the internal opposition rather than on external expansion and most probably will have a short life-term.

Scenario No 3: the liberal-market authoritarianism. The president and his associates try to strengthen, in a decisive way, the executive branch of power for the purpose of speeding up economic reform. They may decide to organize a national referendum on the draft of the new Constitution in which there is no place left for the major existing legislative institution that is the Congress of People's Deputies of the Russian Federation. Control over the Central Bank of Russia is transferred from the parliament to the government. An attempt to demote the speaker of the Supreme Soviet of the Russian Federation Ruslan Khasbulatov is also feasible. In any way, some democratic deputies in the parliament have already openly called for that measure. There is the possibility of calling for elections in the Constituent Assembly, a body which, according to the views of radical democrats, should replace the present parliament.

This alternative would not imply principal changes in domestic or foreign politics, and maybe could even speed up economic reforms. Nevertheless, given the traditions of Russian history, the fragility of democratic changes in the country and the presence of elements of authoritarianism in the current situation, this scenario might mean the beginning of a fundamental breach of the existing balance of powers, the undesirable weakening of the legislative branch, and, finally, the gradual move towards a harsh authoritarian regime. If such a regime is established, it could sacrifice reforms in order to stay in power and to protect what it has introduced.

Also, there are no firm guarantees that the abovementioned referendums and new elections would not bring undesired results for the government. They could show the disapproval of democrats by a substantial part of the Russian society. The referendum might lead to a serious political and constitutional crisis in Russia, and give an additional push to the process of destabilization and disintegration. The opposition's demands of resignation of the president and of his cabinet would then look more plausible.

There is still a probability, though extremely low, of a **military coup (Scenario No 4)**. The essence and consequences of it would actually be the same as of the red-brown alternative, as such a coup could only be reactionary. It is difficult to imagine that an idea to make such a move would occur to the democratically oriented part of the Russian officers. The main reason for the coup could be an extreme worsening of the social and economic situation in the country, especially due to a stopping of big enterprises, closely connected with military production. The driving force of a military coup could become the lumpen part of the working class, a part of peasantry, and a part of the old nomenclatura. The United Opposition, a part of the representatives of the militaryindustrial complex, and of some power structures (security, militia, etc.) will almost definitely support the military coup. The prevention of a disintegration of Russia, social justice, return to the old order in the country, restoration of the Russian (Soviet) Empire would become main slogans of the coup.

It is very likely that the new class of businessmen, democratic forces intelligentsia would again resist the coup, as it already happened in August 1991. In general, given the present complicated situation in the Russian army, it is difficult to imagine a possibility of any coordinated action on a national level by some of the military.

It would be wrong to disregard the possibility of **Scenario No 5, that is of an economic collapse, social chaos and disturbances, and complete disintegration of the country, including the probability of a civil war.** It is quite evident that under such circumstances Russia would face not only an internal, but also an external catastrophe.

And finally, the **Scenario No 6, the regionalization of Russia,** that is, a gradual move towards a loose federation with a minimal role of Moscow as a center. The absolute majority of Russian experts believe that the process of regionalization is a much more powerful challenge for the integrity of Russia than the process of autonomization of national regions. First of all, it is unlikely that all autonomous republics and regions could simultaneously decide to withdraw from the Russian Federation. Secondly, the majority of them, except Karelia, Sakha-Yakutia, Tuva, Buryatia and the Republics of the North Caucases, have no external borders. Thirdly, in the majority of autonomous regions Russians outnumber other nationalities, including the native ones (on positive and negative scenarios of disintegration of Russia chapter 1, part IV).

The trend towards transforming Russia into a loose entity of economically powerful regions can be weakened by elaborating a cohesive regional policy, and by narrowing contradictions and disagreements between different power structures in the center.

It would be wrong to conclude from the previous analysis that there is no way out of the present complicated domestic situation in Russia. Much will depend on the readiness and the will of major political forces in the country to reach compromises in order to save the Russian statehood and to prevent social unrest. The experience of the recent past shows that such compromises are within a grasp of reality.

Scenarios of the Further Evolution of the CIS

First of all, it is necessary to analyze the possibility of a dissolution of the Commonwealth. Hence the **Scenario No 1: Complete disintegration of the CIS under conditions of relative stability.** This scenario may become a reality in case a substantial number of countries (Ukraine,

Armenia, Azerbaijan, Moldova, and Turkmenistan), due to changes of the regimes, or to general disappointment in the effectiveness of the CIS, will start to gradually reduce their level of participation in the Commonwealth, and to reorient their foreign policies on relations with other countries. But most probably, the dissolution of the CIS cannot take place unless Russia causes it. This could happen in case of the highly unlikely coming to power of radical isolationist-minded nationalists (the so-called "Russian Party"), or, which is even more unlikely, of the ultra-radical democrats. Both groups call for the separation of Russia from other republics. The first puts forward xenophobic motives. The second seeks separation due to alleged political backwardness of most republics of the former USSR.

The only probable cause of disintegration is the coming to power in Russia of a new imperialist regime that could try to reintegrate the former USSR by force and would most likely achieve the opposite results. This is **Scenario No 2: the disintegration of the CIS due to the imperial degeneration of the regime in Russia or to the replacement of the current Russian regime by an ultra-conservative one.** A new regime could attempt to restore the Soviet Union, first of all by some sort of annexation of territories, the population of which expressed their wish to join Russia (South Ossetia and Abkhazia). The emergence of the issue of returning to Russia of the Crimean peninsula and of Northern Kazakhstan is also quite probable. Possible consequences of such a policy, implying changes of the present borders within the CIS, are quite evident: the disintegration of the Commonwealth, dramatic deterioration of the relations of Russia with neighboring countries (including even military clashes), failure of economic reforms, resumption of a confrontation of Russia with the West, and most important, the disintegration of the Russian state itself.

Scenario No 3: complete chaos and social disorder on the territory of the former Soviet Union, or at least, on a substantial part of it. Such a cataclysm would be a result, first of all, of a failure of economic reforms in some of the major countries of the CIS (especially in Russia), of a disintegration of Russia, or a fast deterioration of relations between the CIS countries. Such a political "Chernobyl" would lead not only to a final disintegration of the CIS, but also to a multidimensional destabilization on the huge Eurasian territory with unpredictable and most probably catastrophic consequences for the world community.

However, it would be a mistake not to describe the scenarios of survival of the CIS. **Scenario No 4: preserving the Commonwealth on a low level of cooperation,** or more exactly, on a level which is insufficient to meet the demands of a modern society, especially the demands of an economic development of the CIS countries. There is a probability that the parliaments of the countries of the CIS that signed the agreements on collective security, a common currency system and on a coordinated credit and financial policy in recent months will not ratify them or will try to postpone their approval for an indefinite period. This scenario will become a reality, if Russia, Kazakhstan and other leaders of the integration tendency prove to be unable to find ways to build the Commonwealth with Ukraine. While not willing to formally leave the CIS, Kiev is doing everything possible to block its dynamic development.

And finally, the **Scenario No 5: preservation and eventual strengthening of the CIS, but in a modified form,** with one group of countries moving towards a higher level of integration, and another group continuing to participate in those spheres and in such ways which it finds acceptable from the point of view of the respective national interests. Such a core of the CIS is becoming a reality: six countries of the CIS (Russia, Belarus, Kazakhstan, Armenia, Kirghizstan, and Uzbekistan) already claimed their readiness for a closer cooperation in political, military, and financial spheres, and also in the creation of the Parliamentary Assembly of the CIS (chapter 8, part II). A formation of some type of a political union between Russia, Belarus, and so far, essentially, the republics of Central Asia, is, as a whole, in correspondence with the geopolitical interests of Russia. However, such a union would be an additional economic burden for Russia.

It would be wishful thinking to expect, at the present stage of historical development, any wider form of integration on the post-Soviet territory, given the political and psychological attitudes of many present leaders of the CIS countries and the fears of the resumption of the imperial syndrome in the foreign policy of Russia.

The results of the last meeting of the leaders of the CIS countries (October 9, 1992) have reaffirmed such conclusions. Not long before this meeting, the President of Kazakhstan Nursultan Nazarbayev promulgated some concrete proposals that could lead to a higher level of integration within the CIS. He proposed to create the Council for Economic Cooperation, the Banking Union, the Defensive Union, the Economic Court, and also to increase the role of the Parliamentary Assembly of the CIS.

Not one of these proposals was accepted in full, though no one was rejected completely. Russia, for example, was not very enthusiastic about the idea of a Banking Union. As a result of the discussion, the agreement on creating on Interstate Bank was signed by seven countries (Armenia, Belarus, Kazakhstan, Kirghizstan, Moldova, Uzbekistan, and Russia). Agreement on the principles of the creation of a common rouble zone was signed by Russia, Belarus, Uzbekistan, Armenia, Kazakhstan, and Kirghizstan. Mostly due to objections from Ukraine, instead of the Council for Economic Cooperation, the decision to create the Consultative Working Economic Commission was adopted (the commission will be under the auspices of the Council of Heads of States and Heads of Governments of the CIS countries).

In other words, some type of a Commonwealth of different paces may be the only plausible scenario of the development of the CIS in the nearest future.

Conclusion

The highly dynamic development of the processes on the territory of the former USSR does not give a chance to predict the future with any degree of confidence. However, the experts participating in the preparation of the report came to the conclusion that for the coming years the combination of *scenario No 1* from the first set (Russia), and *Scenario No 5* from the second set (the CIS) will be most likely.

One more concluding note. It is relatively obvious that due to the social revolution and especially to the disintegration of the USSR, *the post-Soviet space has entered a prolonged (stretched for a few decades) period of geopolitical instability.*

Managing this instability will become the main challenge for Russia, the CIS, and the whole international community. Recent attitudes in the West show that the latter is not ready to involve itself deeply into managing this instability. New instruments have to be found for that. One of the possible ways is endowing Russia and the CIS with a special role in managing these conflicts under the supervision of the international community, especially the CSCE and the UN.

If some kind of an effective instrument or rather a set of instruments is not found, the former USSR could first plunge back into history and then even degenerate into a "geostrategic hole", i.e. a totally unregulated security space spreading out instability and sucking in neighboring regions. But such a development can and should be prevented.

Tables and Charts

Table 1: Economic potential of the USSR: breakdown by some former union republics and their regional groupings (1990, in percent)

	Russia	Ukraine Belarus Moldova	Kazakhstan Uzbekistan Tajikistan Turkmenistan Kyrgyzstan	Azerbaijan Georgia Armenia	Litva Latvia Estonia
Territory	76.2	3.8	16.9	0.8	0.8
Population	51.3	23.1	17.3	5.5	2.7
National income	61.3	21.7	9.6	3.8	3.2
Industrial prod.	66.4	20.9	6.5	3.7	2.7
Agricultur prod.	46.2	30.6	14.9	3.8	4.5
Import	67.5	18.8	6.5	3.8	3.4
Export	69.7	20.0	6.4	2.0	2.2

Source: Goskomstat SSSR. Narodnoje khoziaistwo SSSR v 1990 g. Moskva. Financy i statistica 1991.

Table 2: The CIS countries: some indicators of economic development in 1991 (1990 = 100)

	National income (produced)*	Retail trade*	Foreign trade turnover	Housing	Whole sale prices	Retail prices
CIS, total	91	91	62	83	238	186
Russia	89	92	63	78	238	184
Ukraine	89	90	58	81	222	183
Belarus	97	97	55	101	251	181
Moldova	88	84	51	82	231	197
Kazakhstan	90	86	61	81	273	183
Uzbekistan	99	91	60	96	248	183
Kirgizstan	96	83	58	82	231	197
Tajikistan	91	79	56	71	263	184
Turkmenistan	99	88	63	117	305	185
Armenia	85	75	78	96	220	191
Azerbaijan	100	87	58	92	235	187

*In constant prices

Source: Ekonomika stran-chlenov SNG 1991. "Ekonomika i zisn", No 6, February 1992, p. 13.

Table 3: "Pyramid of integration" (lowest level of integration at the margins)

Ac-cords	Participants										
	Azerb	Belar	Armen	Kazah	RF	Tadj	Uzb	Kirg	Turkm	Ukr	Mold
1		+	+	+	+	+					
2		+	+	+	+	+	+				
3		+	+	+	+	+	+	+			
4		+	+	+	+	+	+	+	+		
5		+	+	+	+	+	+	+	+	+	
6	+	+	+	+	+	+	+	+	+	+	
7	+	+	+	+	+	+	+	+	+	+	+

Figures in the table mark the following agreements/blocks of agreements with identical voting pattern:
1 – on creating the Ministers of Defense Council (Febr. 1992)
2 – on Collective Security (May 1992), on Joint Forces High Command (March 1992)
3 – on military powers of the CIS supreme bodies: Heads of State, Heads of Government, Defense Ministers Councils (March 1992), on the CIS Joint Armed Forces (March 1992)
4 – on General Purpose Forces (Febr. 1992), on the CIS joint defense budget (Febr. 1992; Azerbijan and Ukraine have agreed to partially finance the Strategic Forces on their territory for a limited period)
5 – on Space Control and Ballistic Missiles Early Warning Systems (July 1992)
6 – on the status of the Strategic Forces (Febr. 1992), on social and legal rights of the servicemen (Febr, 1992), on legal service in the joint and national armed forces, on use of air space (both – May 1992)
7 – on the CIS Strategic Forces (December 1991), on Border Guard Forces (Dec. 1991), on ratification and implementation of arms control agreements (Febr. 1992), on sharing out of the TLE quotas under the CFE Agreement (May 1992).

Sources: Diplomaticheskii vestnik (Diplomatic Herald), 1992, Nos 1, 2–3, 4–5, 7; Armiia (Army), No 10, 1992, p. 34–37; Krasnaia Zvezda Dec.–July 1992; Izvestia, Dec.–July, 1992.

Chart 1: The CIS military security structure

Heads of State Council

C-in-C, CIS Joint Armed Forces

CIS Ministers of Defense Council*

Nuclear Strategy		Planning Group	Secretariat
Strategic Forces Cmnder - SRNF*** - Air-borne Strat. Forces - Sea-based Strat. Forces - Space Defense - Space Control - Nuclear Guardians - Strat. intelligence	Chief of Staff JCS** — — — — — — - Operational Department - Major Dep-t of Mobiliz. and Organizing activities - Personnel Committee - Mil.Technol. Committee - Supplies Committee - Armed Forces Development and Training Committee - Chief of Staff Deputies (republican representatives)	Deputy C-In-C on conflicts resolution — — — — — — - Collective Peace-Keeping Forces - Collective Forces for Local Conflicts Resolution (on external borders) Air Defense Commander Naval Commander	Standing CIS High Command Representative at the Heads of States/ Govern-ts Councils — — — — — — Air Force Commander

* Non-standing
** Joint Chiefs of Staff, Non-standing, representatives of national armed forces
*** Strategic Rocket Nuclear Forces

Source: Izvestia, July 9 1992.

Chart 2: The Proposed Shape of Russia's Armed Forces by the Year 2000

The President, C-in-C

Minister of Defense

General Staff

(Armed Services)

----SDF*----	----Land Forces----	----Navy----
– Ballistic Missile Armies (ICBMs and SLBM**)	– Combined Arms Corps (+Armies?)	– Fleets – Flotillas
– Strategic Aviation	– Military Districts (?)	– Squadrons
– Operational-level Aviation		– Naval bases
– Front-level (tactical) Aviation	– Training Centers	
– Milit.Transport Aviation	– Reserve Forces	
– BMD*** Corps	– National Guard	
– Space Control Corps	– Air Defense missile and radar	
– BMEW**** Corps	(large) units	
– other Space forces		

* Will include fighter-interceptors from the disbanded Air Defense Service.
** Intercontinental Ballistic Missiles, Sea-Launched Ballistic Missiles
*** Ballistic Missile Defense
**** Ballistic Missile Early Warning System

Source: Voennaia Misl, Special edition, July 1992, p. 52.

The Author

Prof. Dr. Sergei A. Karaganov
Deputy Director of the Institute of Europe, Russian Academy of Science. Born 12. September 1952 in Moscow; 1969–1974 study of economics at Moscow Lomonosov University, 1974–1988 successively Ph. D. candidate, Assistant and Head of department of the USA and Canada Institute of the Academy of Science; Ph. D. in economics 1979, Ph. D. in Political Science 1989. Since April 1989 Deputy Director of the Institute of Europe.

Publications: i.a.
Die vernünftigen Hinlänglichkeiten und neues politisches Denken, Moskau 1989 (co-author); Europa und die Sowjetunion, Moskau 1991; The Year of Europe: a Soviet view, Survival, March/April 1990; Security Implication of the Soviet Future, in: Global Responsibilites: Europe in Tomorrow's World, Gütersloh 1991.

The Project Partners

The Bertelsmann Foundation sees itself as an institution which, in line with the mandate and principles laid down in its constitution, is committed to promoting innovation, generating ideas and, above all, helping to move pressing problems closer to a solution an injecting important issues into a broadly based discussion.

It is with these objectives in mind that the Bertelsmann Foundation initiated the project "Strategies and Options for the Future of Europe". It is designed to make a contribution in conceptual, contentual and material terms to the solution of European political problems in the present and the future. At the same time the project is intended to improve understanding between European countries and to strengthen the process of integration in Europe while preserving national and regional cultural identities. To give the project the necessary conceptual guidance the Bertelsmann Foundation nominated an international advisory council composed of high-ranking experts in the field of politics, economics and science. The public is kept informed about the results of the project work by, among others, two series of publications: the "Basic Findings", and the "Working Papers".

Responsibility for the scientific tasks in developing, implementing and communicating the project objectives was assumed by the *Research Group on European Affairs* within the Institute of Political Science at the Johannes Gutenberg Universität in Mainz. In doing so the group can fall back on more than ten years of intensive research into European issues conducted at the Institute of Political Science. A diversity of publications, among them the editorial responsibility for the "Mainzer Beiträge zur Europäischen Einigung" and cooperation on the "Jahrbuch der Europäischen Integration" are ample evidence of this work. What is more, the Research Group on European Affairs possesses a comprehensive infrastructure. This includes not only two editorial teams but also a research library and the European Documentation Center that has on file all documents and publications of the organs of the European Community and is connected to the European data base network.

The Publications

As a direct outcome of the work on the project "Strategies and Options for the Future of Europe" the publications listed in the following have so far been issued:

Information on the approach, the objectives, the fields of work:
Bertelsmann-Stiftung (ed.), **Strategien und Optionen für die Zukunft Europas. Ziele und Konturen eines Projektes.** Gütersloh 1988, 23 p.
Bertelsmann Foundation (ed.), **Strategies and Options for the Future of Europe.** Aims and Contours of a Project. Gütersloh 1989, 23 p.
Fondation Bertelsmann (ed.), **Stratégies et options pour l'avenir de l'Europe.** Objectifs et countours d'un project. Gütersloh, 23 p.

In the series "Basic Findings" (Bertelsmann Foundation Publishing):
Forschungsgruppe Europa, **Europäische Defizite, europäische Perspektiven – eine Bestandsaufnahme für morgen.** Grundlagen 1. Gütersloh 1988. 222 p. ISBN 3-89204-011-7. DM 20.00.
Research Group on European Affairs, **European Deficits, European Perspectives – Taking Stock for Tomorrow.** Basic Findings 1. Gütersloh 1989. 232 p., ISBN 3-89204-018-4. DM 20.00.
Rolf H. Hasse, **Die Europäische Zentralbank: Perspektiven für eine Weiterentwicklung des Europäischen Währungssystems.** Grundlagen 2. Gütersloh 1989. 257 p., ISBN 3-89204-036-2. DM 20.00.
Wolfgang Däubler, **Sozialstaat EG? Die andere Dimension des Binnenmarktes.** Grundlagen 3. Gütersloh 1989. 214 p., ISBN 3-89204-026-5. DM 20.00.
Wolfgang Däubler, **Market and Social Justice in the EC – the Other Dimension of the Internal Market.** Basic Findings 3. Gütersloh 1991, ISBN 3-89204-041-9. DM 20.00.
Dieter Biehl, Horst Winter, **Europa finanzieren – ein föderalistisches Modell. Strategien und Optionen für die Zukunft Europas.** Grundlagen 4. Gütersloh 1990, 175 p., ISBN 3-89204-028-1. DM 20.00.

Bertelsmann Stiftung (ed.), **Die Zukunft Europas – Kultur und Verfassung des Kontinents.** Grundlagen 5. Gütersloh 1991. 333 p., ISBN 3-89204-048-6. DM 20.00.
Lutz Wicke, Burckhard Huckestein, **Umwelt Europa – der Ausbau zur ökologischen Marktwirtschaft.** Grundlagen 6. Gütersloh 1991. 256 p., ISBN 3-89204-049-4. DM 20.00.
Werner Weidenfeld, Josef Janning (eds.), **Global Responsibilities: Europe in Tomorrow's World.** Basic Findings 7. Gütersloh 1991. 240 p., ISBN 3-89204-053-2. DM 20.00.
Kenneth Button, **Europäische Verkehrspolitik – Wege in die Zukunft.** Grundlagen 8. Gütersloh 1992. 192 p., ISBN 3-89204-055-9. DM 20.00.
Klaus W. Grewlich, **Europa im globalen Technologiewettlauf: Der Weltmarkt wird zum Binnenmarkt.** Grundlagen 9. Gütersloh 1992. 352 p. ISBN 3-89204-054-0. DM 20.00.
Reinhard Rupprecht, Markus Hellenthal, **Innere Sicherheit im Europäischen Binnenmarkt.** Grundlagen 10. Gütersloh 1992. 392 p. ISBN 3-89204-058-3. DM 20.00.
Werner Weidenfeld (ed.), **Herausforderung Mittelmeer: Aufgaben, Ziele und Strategien europäischer Politik.** Grundlagen 11. Gütersloh 1992. 244 p., ISBN 3-89204-063-X.

In the series "Working Papers" (Bertelsmann Foundation Publishers):
Forschungsgruppe Europa (ed.), **Binnenmarkt '92: Perspektiven aus deutscher Sicht.** Arbeitspapiere 1. Gütersloh 1988, 4th ed. 1989, 222 p., ISBN 3-89204-015-X. DM 12.00.
Werner Weidenfeld, Walther Stützle, Curt Gasteyger, Josef Janning, **Die Architektur europäischer Sicherheit: Probleme, Kriterien, Perspektiven.** Arbeitspapiere 2. Gütersloh 1989. 73 p., ISBN 3-89204-020-6. DM 12.00.
Bertelsmann Stiftung (ed.), **Die Vollendung des Europäischen Währungssystems.** Arbeitspapiere 3. Gütersloh 1989. 72 p., ISBN 3-89204-024-9. DM 12.00.
Werner Weidenfeld, Josef Janning, **Der Umbruch Europas: Die Zukunft des Kontinents.** Arbeitspapiere 4. Gütersloh 1990. 71 p., ISBN 3-89204-032-X. DM 12.00.
Werner Weidenfeld, Walther Stützle, **Abschied von der alten Ordnung. Europas neue Sicherheit.** Arbeitspapiere 5. Gütersloh 1990. 44 p., ISBN 3-89204-032-X. DM 12.00.
Werner Weidenfeld, Christine Holeschovsky, Elmar Brok, Fritz Franzmeier, Dieter Schumacher, Jürgen Klose, **Die doppelte Integration: Europa und das größere Deutschland.** Arbeitspapiere 6. Gütersloh 1991. 109 p., ISBN 3-89204-042-7. DM 12.00.

Werner Weidenfeld, **Wie Europa verfaßt sein soll. Materialien zur Politischen Union.** Arbeitspapiere 7. Gütersloh 1991. 458 p., ISBN 3-89204-045-1. DM 12.00.
Werner Weidenfeld, Manfred Huterer, **Osteuropa: Herausforderungen – Probleme – Strategien.** Arbeitspapiere 8. Gütersloh 1992. 112 p., ISBN 3-89204-059-1. DM 12.00.
Werner Weidenfeld, Manfred Huterer, **Eastern Europe: Challenges – Problems – Strategies.** Working Papers 8. Gütersloh 1993. 103 p. ISBN 3-89204-074-5. DM 12.00.
Werner Weidenfeld (ed.), **Was ändert die Einheit?.** Arbeitspapiere 9. Gütersloh 1993. 138 p. ISBN 3-89204-069-9. DM 12.00.
Georg Brunner, **Nationalitätenprobleme und Minderheitenkonflikte in Osteuropa.** Arbeitspapiere 10. Gütersloh 1993. 143 p. ISBN 3-89204-071-0. DM 12.00.
Werner Weidenfeld (ed.), **Der vollendete Binnenmarkt – eine Herausforderung für die Europäische Gemeinschaft.** Arbeitspapiere 11. Gütersloh 1993. 152 p., ISBN 3-89204-072-9. DM 12,00.
Werner Weidenfeld, Josef Janning (eds.), **Europe in Global Change.** Gütersloh 1993. 288 p. ISBN 3-89204-084-2. DM 34,00.